S E R I E S

A life-changing encounter
with God's Word from the books of the

MINOR
PROPHETS 2
NAHUM, HABAKKUK, ZEPHANIAH,
HAGGAI, ZECHARIAH & MALACHI

*A NavPress published resource in alliance
with Tyndale House Publishers, Inc.*

NAVPRESS◐

NavPress is the publishing ministry of The Navigators, an international Christian organization and leader in personal spiritual development. NavPress is committed to helping people grow spiritually and enjoy lives of meaning and hope through personal and group resources that are biblically rooted, culturally relevant, and highly practical.

For more information, visit www.NavPress.com.

CONTENTS

HOW TO USE THIS GUIDE

Along with all the volumes in the LIFECHANGE series of Bible studies, the two guides to the Minor Prophets (Nahum through Malachi in this second volume; Hosea through Micah in the first) share common goals:

1. To provide you a firm foundation of understanding, plus a thirst to return to the Minor Prophets throughout your life.

2. To give you study patterns and skills that help you explore every part of the Bible.

3. To offer you historical background, word definitions, and explanation notes to aid your study.

4. To help you grasp as a whole the message of each of the Minor Prophets.

5. To teach you how to let God's Word transform you into Christ's image.

As you begin

This guide includes twelve lessons that will take you chapter by chapter through the last six of the Minor Prophets. Each lesson is designed to take from one to two hours of preparation to complete on your own. To benefit most from this time, here's a good way to begin your work on each lesson:

1. Pray for God's help to keep you mentally alert and spiritually sensitive.

2. Read attentively through the entire passage mentioned in the lesson's title. (You may want to read the passage from two or more Bible versions—perhaps at least once from a more literal translation such as the New International Version, English Standard Version, New American Standard Bible, or New King James Version, and perhaps once more in a paraphrase such as *The Message* or the New Living Translation.) Do your reading in an environment that's as free as possible from distractions. Allow your mind and heart to meditate on these words you encounter, words that are God's personal gift to you and to all His people.

After reading the passage, you're ready to dive into the numbered questions in this guide that make up the main portion of each lesson. Each of these questions is followed by blank space for writing your answers. (This act of writing your answers helps clarify your thinking and stimulates your mental engagement with the passage, as well as your later recall.) Use extra paper or a notebook if the space for recording your answers seems too cramped. Continue through the questions in numbered order. If any question seems too difficult or unclear, just skip it and go on to the next.

Each of these questions will typically direct you to the text of one of the Minor Prophets to look again at a certain portion of the assigned passage for that lesson. (At this point, be sure to use a more literal Bible translation, rather than a paraphrase.)

As you look closer at this passage, it's helpful to approach it in this progression:

Observe. What does the passage actually *say*? Ask God to help you see it clearly. Notice everything that's there.

Interpret. What does the passage *mean*? Ask God to help you understand. And remember that any passage's meaning is fundamentally determined by its *context*. So stay alert to all you'll see about the setting and background of the Minor Prophets, and keep thinking of these books as a whole while you proceed through them chapter by chapter. You'll be progressively building up your insights and familiarity with what they're all about.

Apply. Keep asking yourself, *How does this truth affect my life?* (Pray for God's help as you examine yourself in light of that truth, and in light of His purpose for each passage.)

Try to consciously follow all three of these approaches as you shape your written answer to each question in the lesson.

The extras

In addition to the numbered questions you see in this guide, each lesson also offers several optional questions or suggestions that appear in the margins. All of these will appear under one of three headings:

Optional Application. These are suggested options for application. Consider these with prayerful sensitivity to the Lord's guidance.

For Thought and Discussion. Many of these questions address various ethical issues and other biblical principles that lead to a wide range of implications. They tend to be particularly suited for group discussions.

For Further Study. These often include cross-references to other parts of the Bible that shed light on a topic in the lesson, plus questions that delve deeper into the passage.

(For additional help for more effective Bible study, refer to the "Study Aids" section on page 151.)

6

Changing your life

Don't let your study become an exercise in knowledge alone. Recognize the passage as *God's* Word, and stay in dialogue with Him as you study. Pray, "Lord, what do You want me to notice here?" "Father, why is this true?" "Lord, how does my life measure up to this?"

Let biblical truth sink into your inner convictions so you'll increasingly be able to act on this truth as a natural way of living.

At times you may want to consider memorizing a certain verse or passage you come across in your study, one that particularly challenges or encourages you. To help with that, write the words on a card to keep with you, and set aside a few minutes each day to think about the passage. Recite it to yourself repeatedly, always thinking about its meaning. Return to it as often as you can, for a brief review. You'll soon find the words coming to mind spontaneously, and they'll begin to shape your motives and actions.

For group study

Exploring Scripture together in a group is especially valuable for the encouragement, support, and accountability it provides as you seek to apply God's Word to your life. Together you can listen jointly for God's guidance, pray for each other, help one another resist temptation, and share the spiritual principles you're practicing. Together you affirm that growing in faith, hope, and love is important, and that *you need each other* in the process.

A group of four to ten people allows for the closest understanding of each other and the richest discussions in Bible study, but you can adapt this guide for groups of other sizes. It will suit a wide range of group types, such as home Bible studies, growth groups, youth groups, and church classes. Both new and mature Christians will benefit from the guide, regardless of their previous experience in Bible study.

Aim for a positive atmosphere of acceptance, honesty, and openness. In your first meeting, explore candidly everyone's expectations and goals for your time together.

A typical schedule for group study is to take one lesson per week, but feel free to split lessons if you want to discuss them more thoroughly. Or omit some questions in a lesson if your preparation or discussion time is limited. (You can always return to this guide later for further study on your own.)

When you come together, you probably won't have time to discuss all the questions in the lesson, so it's helpful to choose ahead of time the ones you want to make sure and cover thoroughly. This is one of the main responsibilities a group leader typically assumes.

Each lesson in this guide ends with a section called "For the group." It suggests how to focus the discussion, how to apply the lesson to daily life, and so on. Reading each lesson's "For the group" section ahead of time can help the leader be more effective in guiding the group.

You'll get the greatest benefit from your time together if each group member prepares by writing out his or her answers to each question in the

7

lesson. The private reflection and prayer that this preparation can stimulate will be especially important in helping everyone discern how God wants you to apply each lesson to your daily life.

What to do in your time together

There are many ways to structure the group meeting, and you may want to vary your routine occasionally to help keep things fresh.

Here are some of the elements you can consider including as you come together for each lesson:

Pray together. It's good to pause for prayer as you begin your time together, as well as to incorporate a later more extensive time of prayer for each other, after you've had time to share personal needs and prayer requests. (You may want to record these in a notebook.) When you begin with prayer, it's worthwhile and honoring to God to ask especially for His Holy Spirit's guidance of your time together.

Worship. Some groups like to sing together and worship God with prayers of praise.

Review. You may want to take time to discuss what difference the previous week's lesson has made in your life, as well as recall the major emphasis you discovered in the passage for that week.

Read the passage aloud. Once you're ready to focus attention together on the assigned Scripture passage in the week's lesson, read it aloud. (One person could do this, or the reading could be shared.)

Open up for lingering questions. Allow time for the group members to mention anything in the passage that they may have particular questions about.

Summarize the passage. Have one or two persons offer a summary of what the passage covers.

Discuss. This will be the heart of your time together and will likely take the biggest portion of your time. Focus on the questions you see as the most important and most helpful. Allow and encourage everyone to be part of the discussion on each question. You may want to take written notes as the discussion proceeds. Ask follow-up questions to sharpen your attention and to deepen your understanding of what you discuss. You may want to give special attention to the questions in the margin under the heading "For Thought and Discussion." Remember that sometimes these can be especially good for discussion, but be prepared for different answers and opinions. As you hear each other, keep in mind each other's various backgrounds, personalities, and ways of thinking. You can practice godly discernment without ungodly judgment in your discussion.

Encourage further personal study. You can find more opportunities for exploring the lesson's themes and issues under the marginal heading "For Further Study" throughout the lesson. You can also pursue some of these together, during your group time.

Focus on application. Look especially at the "Optional Application" items listed in the margins throughout the lesson. Keep encouraging one another in the continual work of adjusting your lives to the truths God gives you in Scripture.

Summarize your discoveries. You may want to read aloud through the passage one last time together, using this opportunity to solidify your understanding and appreciation of it, and to clarify how the Lord is speaking to you through it.

Look ahead. Glance together at the headings and questions in the next lesson to see what's coming next.

Give thanks to God. It's good to end your time together by pausing to express gratitude to God for His Word and for the work of His Spirit in your minds and hearts during your time together.

Get to know each other better. In early sessions together, you may want to spend time establishing trust, common ground, and a sense of each other's background and what each person hopes to gain from the study. This may help you later with honest discussion on how the Bible applies to each of you. Understanding each other better will make it easier to share about personal applications.

Keep these worthy guidelines in mind throughout your time together:

Let us consider how we may spur one another on toward love and good deeds.

(HEBREWS 10:24)

Carry each other's burdens, and in this way you will fulfill the law of Christ.

(GALATIANS 6:2)

Accept one another, then, just as Christ accepted you, in order to bring praise to God.

(ROMANS 15:7)

THE MINOR PROPHETS

Major Messages from Across the Centuries

The six books you'll focus on in this study represent the concluding portion of the final twelve books in our Old Testament. All twelve of them have together been grouped and perceived as a collective unit for millennia (as discussed more fully in the introduction to the first of these two LIFECHANGE volumes concerning the Minor Prophets). As we observed there, all of these twelve books "have their distinctive features, so there is no sense of monotony as we move from one to the next."[1]

A few more observations:

"The Minor Prophets seem to have been preoccupied with nations and events that have little relevance to today's world. How unlike the New Testament they are! A careful study of these prophets, however, reveals that many of the themes they expound transit the Testaments. They speak of the love of God as well as his justice. Their prophecies are not all doom, but are often rich with hope. . . .

"Anyone who turns from reading the Minor Prophets hearing only words of recrimination and judgment has not read them fairly. Within the dismal events these prophets describe lurks the hand of God, and beyond these events is the bright prospect of a kingdom inaugurated by One whom Zechariah portrays as suffering betrayal, piercing, and eventual death. The Minor Prophets are not as time-bound as we may think."[2]

Timeline

Following is a suggested chronology for these last six of the Minor Prophets.[3] (The dating for some of these books is uncertain.)

Nahum (in the reign of Hezekiah of Judah) — between 710 and 699 BC
Habakkuk (in the reign of Manasseh or Josiah of Judah) — between 650 and 628 BC

Zephaniah (in the reign of Josiah of Judah)—between 628 and 623 BC
Haggai (in the reign of Darius of Persia)—in 520 BC
Zechariah (in the reign of Darius of Persia)—between 520 and 480 BC
Malachi (in the reign of Artaxerxes of Persia)—between 433 and 424 BC

1. Leland Ryken and Philip Graham Ryken, eds., *The Literary Study Bible* (Wheaton, IL: Crossway, 2007), introduction to Habakkuk, "The book at a glance."
2. Thomas Edward McComiskey, ed., *The Minor Prophets* (Grand Rapids, MI: Baker, 2009), ix.
3. Adapted from C. F. Keil and F. Delitzsch, *Commentary on the Old Testament: The Minor Prophets*, vol. 10 (Edinburgh, UK: Clark, 1871; Peabody, MA: Hendrickson, 1996), 3.

NAHUM

God's Judgment Against Nineveh

"While most Old Testament prophetic books predict God's judgment against Israel and Judah, the prophecy in Nahum is directed against Nineveh, capital city and representative of the nation of Assyria. Because Assyria was a wicked nation, noted especially for its cruelty in warfare, the prophet makes no apology for predicting its destruction. He throws himself into his denunciation of Nineveh with enthusiasm and a taunting tone. . . . What Nahum utters against Nineveh is God's message to all evil nations."[1]

"*Nahum* means 'comfort' or 'consolation' (of God). This is very thought-provoking since Nahum's entire message concerns the destruction of Nineveh. . . .

"Nahum prophesied . . . around 620 B.C., about the time of Habakkuk, Zephaniah, and the early part of Jeremiah's ministry. . . .

"Nahum's book . . . provided answers to the questions of God's people: 'Has God forsaken us? Why are the Assyrians prospering? Are God's promises empty?' Nahum affirms that God may be 'slow to anger,' but He 'will not at all acquit the wicked' (1:3). Moreover, God is indeed 'a stronghold in the day of trouble' (1:7). This is also a vital message for today — in the press of circumstances and misfortune, God's people are prone to forget that God is in control."[2]

"As a true prophet of Yahweh, Nahum was profoundly aware that the Lord, the incomparable and all-powerful God, held universal dominion over the kingdoms of this world. Like his predecessor Isaiah, Nahum was also a gifted poet. Using a wealth of imagery and pictorial language, the prophet portrays the total destruction of Nineveh by an anonymous enemy, and so voices the universal relief and joy of all who suffered under the oppressive regime of a merciless tyrant."[3]

1. For getting the most from the books of the Minor Prophets, one of the best guidelines is found in 2 Timothy 3:16-17, words which Paul wrote with the Old Testament first in view. He said that *all* Scripture is of great benefit to (a) teach us, (b) rebuke us, (c) correct us, and (d) train us in righteousness. Paul added that these Scriptures completely equip the person of God "for every good work." As you think seriously about those guidelines, in which of these areas do you especially want to experience the usefulness of the books of Nahum, Habakkuk, Zephaniah, Haggai,

Zechariah, and Malachi? Express your desire in a written prayer to God.

_____

_____

_____

_____

2. Think also about these words of Paul to Timothy: "Do your best to present yourself to God as one approved, a worker who does not need to be ashamed and who correctly handles the word of truth" (2 Timothy 2:15). As you study God's Word of Truth in these final six books of the Old Testament, the Lord calls you to be a "worker." It takes *work*—concentration and persever-ance—to fully appropriate God's blessings for us in this book. Express here your commitment before God to work diligently in this study of the last six books in the Minor Prophets.

_____

_____

_____

_____

3. Glance ahead through the pages of Nahum and briefly scan all three chapters. What are your overall impressions of the book, including its structure and its themes?

_____

_____

_____

_____

4. Now turn your focus to the first chapter of Nahum. What are the great truths about God that are evident in these passages?

Optional Application: After His resurrection, when Jesus was explaining Old Testament passages to His disciples, we read that He "opened their minds so they could understand the Scriptures" (Luke 24:45). Ask God to do that kind of work in *your* mind as you study the book of Nahum, so you're released and free to learn everything here He wants you to learn — and so you can become as bold and worshipful and faithful as those early disciples of Jesus. Express this desire to Him in prayer.

For Thought and Discussion: How familiar is the book of Nahum to you? What have been your previous impressions of this book?

15

Optional Application: The prophet's words of praise for God in Nahum 1:7 occur in a message of great judgment against an ungodly power. What personal encouragement do the words of praise in Nahum 1:7 bring to you, especially in light of the evil in today's world?

Nahum 1:2-5

_____

_____

_____

Nahum 1:6-9

_____

_____

_____

Prophecy (1:1). Or "burden" (NKJV). See also Isaiah 13:1; 17:1; Habakkuk 1:1; Zechariah 9:1; 12:1; Malachi 1:1. "The Hebrew for this word is related to a Hebrew verb meaning 'to lift up, carry' and is possibly to be understood as either lifting up one's voice or carrying a burden. Such an 'oracle' often contains a message of doom."[4]

Jealous (1:2). "The emphasis is on God's desire for righteousness."[5]

Bashan . . . Carmel . . . Lebanon (1:4). "These three places were noted for their fertility, vineyards, and trees."[6]

The Lord is good (1:7). "Even in the manifestation of His wrath God proves His goodness. . . . The goodness of the Lord is seen in the fact that He is a refuge in distress."[7]

5. What do we learn about the Lord's enemies in 1:8-11?

_____

_____

_____

_____

16

Overwhelming flood (1:8). "Symbolic of an invading army (see Isaiah 8:7-8)."[8]

6. What significance do you see in the Lord's promise to His people in 1:12-13?

_____

_____

_____

7. What is the emphasis in the message to Nineveh (or, in particular, Assyria's ruler) in 1:14?

_____

_____

_____

You (1:14). The NIV here adds "Nineveh" in brackets. The pronoun here "is masculine singular in Hebrew. Nahum suddenly switches to directly addressing the Assyrian king(s): the Assyrian monarchy would come to a decisive end."[9]

8. What is the emphasis in the message to the Lord's people in 1:15?

_____

_____

_____

9. What does the first chapter of Nahum reveal most about God's heart and character?

_____

_____

_____

In the second chapter of Nahum, "the focus falls on Nineveh. Nahum's prediction reads like an eyewitness account of the city being attacked, overrun by the enemy, and plundered."[10]

10. In the battle description that unfolds in Nahum's second chapter, what images impress you most, and what do they bring to mind for you?

_____

_____

_____

_____

11. What reason for the Lord's judgment against Nineveh is given in 2:2, and what significance do you see in this?

_____

_____

_____

_____

Red . . . scarlet (2:3). "These terms emphasize the awe-inspiring appearance of the approaching army, whether the color refers to their actual robes or to the blood stains on them."[11]

12. How is the battle's onslaught portrayed in 2:3-5?

_____

_____

_____

_____

13. How are Nineveh's failing defenses portrayed in 2:6-10?

_____

_____

_____

River gates (2:6). "Nineveh was located on the bank of the Tigris River, and a smaller river flowed through the city. Conflicting ancient accounts ascribe the fall of Nineveh to flooding when the enemy redirected the dams and sluices of the water system."[12]

14. In 2:11-12, what is the effect of the lion imagery and what it says about Nineveh?

_____

_____

_____

Lion and lioness (2:11). "The Assyrian kings exhibited ferocity in their attacking and 'devouring' other lands, and called themselves lions."[13]

15. What is the emphasis in the Lord's message of judgment in 2:13, and how does it serve as a focal point for chapter 2?

_____

_____

_____

_____

_____

19

For Thought and Discussion: What does the book of Nahum reveal about God's general attitude toward nations that are ruthlessly aggressive? And how might this message apply to some of the world's nations today?

For Further Study: Nineveh is on center stage in two short books of the Bible — Jonah and Nahum. What contrasts do you see in the perspectives that these two books give us concerning Nineveh?

In the final chapter of Nahum, "the various parts all contribute to its literary unity, and together they emphasize the irreversible doom of Nineveh. The prophet . . . places the fate of Nineveh in a universal perspective."[14]

16. As the battle descriptions continue in Nahum 3:1-3, what images impress you most, and what do they bring to mind for you?

_____

_____

_____

_____

17. What is the essence of the charge against Nineveh in 3:4?

_____

_____

_____

18. What is the emphasis in the Lord's message to Nineveh in 3:5-7, and how does it serve as a focal point for chapter 3?

_____

_____

_____

_____

19. For comparison with Nineveh, what is the main truth about Thebes given in 3:8-10?

_____

_____

_____

_____

Put and Libya (3:9). Put is "a neighbor of Egypt, but its location is uncertain."[15]

20. As the battle descriptions continue in 3:11-15, what images impress you most, and what do they bring to mind for you?

_____

_____

_____

_____

21. What are the main points being made in the imagery of the locusts and grasshoppers in 3:15-17?

_____

_____

_____

22. What is the final emphasis of the book in 3:18-19?

_____

_____

_____

_____

Who has not felt your endless cruelty? (3:19). Nahum and Jonah are the only books in the Bible that end with a question. Both books focus on the powerful Assyrian city of Nineveh.

"Although most Old Testament books end with a vision of blessing, the book of Nahum omits that conventional ending."[16]

Optional Application: In what ways do you recognize that the prophecies in the book of Nahum will reach their complete fulfillment only at the second coming of our Lord Jesus Christ? And what relevance does this fact have for your own life in this world?

For Thought and Discussion: Here in Nahum, what do you think accounts for the intensity of the Lord's language against Nineveh?

For Further Study: Scan the messages of judgment against ungodly nations that we find in such passages as Isaiah 13–23, Jeremiah 46–51, Amos 1–2, and Obadiah. What similarities to Nahum do you find in those passages?

23. In your study of the book of Nahum, what have you learned most and appreciated most?

_____

_____

_____

24. What would you select as the key verse or passage in Nahum—one that best captures or reflects the dynamics of what this book is all about?

_____

_____

_____

25. What does the book of Nahum communicate most to you about the heart and character of God?

_____

_____

_____

_____

26. List any lingering questions you have about the book of Nahum.

_____

_____

_____

27. Because all of Scripture testifies ultimately of Christ, where does *Jesus* come most in focus for you in this book?

_____

_____

_____

_____

28. In Romans 15:4, Paul reminds us that the Old Testament Scriptures can give us endurance and perseverance on one hand, as well as comfort and encouragement on the other. In your own life, how do you see the book of Nahum living up to Paul's description? In what ways do the Scriptures help to meet your personal needs for both *perseverance* and *encouragement*?

_____

_____

_____

_____

Optional Application: Which verse or verses in the book of Nahum would be most helpful for you to memorize so you have them always available in your mind and heart for the Holy Spirit to use?

For the group

(In your first meeting, it may be helpful to turn to the front of this book and review together the section titled "How to Use This Guide" on pages 5–9.)

You may want to focus your discussion for lesson 1 especially on the following issues, themes, and concepts, which are recognized as major overall themes in Nahum. How do you see these being dealt with in this book?

- God's justice
- God's anger against evil
- The moral responsibility of nations
- God's omnipotence

The following numbered questions in lesson 1 may stimulate your best and most helpful discussion: 3, 9, 23, 24, 25, 26, 27, and 28.

Look also at the questions in the margins under the heading "For Thought and Discussion."

1. Leland Ryken and Philip Graham Ryken, eds., *The Literary Study Bible* (Wheaton, IL: Crossway, 2007), introduction to Nahum, "The book at a glance."

2. Warren Baker, ed., *The Complete Word Study Old Testament* (Chattanooga, TN: AMG, 1994), introduction to Nahum.

3. *New Geneva Study Bible* (Nashville: Thomas Nelson, 1995), introduction to Nahum, "Author."
4. *NIV Study Bible* (Grand Rapids, MI: Zondervan, 1985), at Isaiah 13:1.
5. *Complete Word Study Old Testament,* at Nahum 1:2,3.
6. *NIV Study Bible*, at Nahum 1:4.
7. C. F. Keil and F. Delitzsch, *Commentary on the Old Testament: The Minor Prophets*, vol. 10 (Edinburgh, UK: Clark, 1871; Peabody, MA: Hendrickson, 1996), 359.
8. *NIV Study Bible*, at Nahum 1:8.
9. *ESV Study Bible* (Wheaton, IL: Crossway, 2008), at Nahum 1:14.
10. *ESV Study Bible*, at Nahum 2:1-13.
11. *New Geneva Study Bible*, at Nahum 2:3.
12. *New Geneva Study Bible*, at Nahum 2:6.
13. *ESV Study Bible*, at Nahum 2:11-12.
14. *New Geneva Study Bible*, at Nahum 3:1-19.
15. *NIV Study Bible*, at Nahum 3:9.
16. Ryken and Ryken, introduction to Nahum, "The book at a glance."

HABAKKUK 1–2
Asking God Why

"Habakkuk is the prophet who asked two questions that God answered at length, and who then responded with a great prayer testifying to his faith in God. More specifically, the prophet expresses questions and doubts regarding God's justice and management of the world."[1]

"Prophets were not only inspired preachers of divine messages to the people of God; they also shared the Lord's burden for His broken world and His deep concern for His wayward people. In this respect, Habakkuk closely resembles Jeremiah. But even more than with Jeremiah, Habakkuk's dialogue with God and his persistent prayers take the place of prophetic preaching as the heart of the message."[2]

The various sections of dialogue in this book may be "representative of Habakkuk's spiritual struggles over a long period of time, possibly beginning as early as 626 [BC] and continuing as late as 590 or after."[3] Habakkuk "asked some of the most penetrating questions in all literature, and the answers are basic to a proper view of God and his relation to history."[4]

"Very little is known about Habakkuk except his name, which means either 'the embracer' or 'the wrestler.' These meanings correspond to Habakkuk's 'wrestling' with the question of why God would let evil go unpunished and then why He would bring calamity on His own people (1:13), while at the same time he 'embraced' by faith the salvation of the LORD (3:18). . . .

"The inquiries that Habakkuk made of God have been echoed by many of God's children down through the ages. The answers he received conclusively affirm that God is not accountable to any man. He is in no way obligated to comply with man's ideas of how He should handle situations. . . . The Lord reminds Habakkuk that God is completely wise and sovereign in all His dealings with men."[5]

1. In Jeremiah 23:29, God says that His Word is "like fire" and "like a hammer." He can use the Scriptures to burn away unclean thoughts and desires in our hearts. He can also use Scripture, with hammer-like hardness, to crush and crumble our spiritual hardness. As you study Habakkuk, how do you most want to see the fire-and-hammer power of God's Word at

work in your own life? Express this longing in a written prayer to God.

_____

_____

_____

_____

2. Glance ahead through the pages of Habakkuk and briefly scan all three chapters. What are your overall impressions of the book, including its structure and its themes?

_____

_____

_____

_____

3. Now turn your focus to the first chapter of Habakkuk.

a. Explain in your own words the issue that concerns the prophet Habakkuk, as expressed in 1:2-4.

_____

_____

_____

b. How do these verses indicate Habakkuk's faith?

_____

_____

_____

4. Summarize the Lord's response to Habakkuk as seen in 1:5-11.

_____

_____

Optional Application: After His resurrection, when Jesus was explaining Old Testament passages to His disciples, we read that He "opened their minds so they could understand the Scriptures" (Luke 24:45). Ask God to do that kind of work in *your* mind as you study the book of Habakkuk so you're released and free to learn everything here He wants you to learn — and so you can become as bold and worshipful and faithful as those early disciples of Jesus. Express this desire to Him in prayer.

For Thought and Discussion: How familiar is the book of Habakkuk to you? What have been your previous impressions of this book?

For Further Study: How does Habakkuk's "How long . . . ?" lament (beginning in 1:2) compare with similar laments in these passages: Psalm 6:3; 13:1-2; 80:4; 89:46; Jeremiah 12:4; Zechariah 1:12.

For Thought and Discussion: In Habakkuk 1:5, the Lord tells His people to "look" and to "be utterly amazed" at the work He intends to do. Is there anything God is doing today in the world that you find utterly amazing?

For Further Study: In Acts 13:40-41, notice how Paul quotes Habakkuk 1:5 as he speaks in the synagogue at Pisidian Antioch. Review the gospel context for these words in Acts 13:32-33 and 13:38-41. What do you find notably appropriate about Paul using this Old Testament verse in this context?

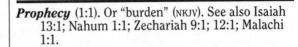

Prophecy (1:1). Or "burden" (NKJV). See also Isaiah 13:1; Nahum 1:1; Zechariah 9:1; 12:1; Malachi 1:1.

The prophet (1:1). "Prophets do not typically use the term 'prophet' for themselves, but Habakkuk is called a prophet twice (1:1; 3:1), possibly because his message differs significantly from that of most other prophets."[6] "Habakkuk was unique among the prophets because he did not speak for God to the people but rather spoke to God about his people and nation."[7]

Violence! (1:2). The Hebrew word "denotes flagrant violation of moral law by which man injures primarily his fellowman. Its underlying meaning is one of ethical wrong, of which physical brutality is only one possible expression."[8] "At this time Judah was probably under King Jehoiakim, who was ambitious, cruel, and corrupt. Habakkuk describes the social corruption and spiritual apostasy of Judah in the late seventh century B.C."[9]

Look (1:5). "This verse is addressed to a plural audience. The hearers, by implication Judeans, are treated as distinct from the 'nations' (or Gentiles), at whom they are to 'look.'"[10]

I am going to do something (1:5). Or more literally, "I am doing a work" (ESV) or "I will work a work" (NKJV). "The 'work' that God would perform among them was their captivity in Babylon. God placed them in exile to purify them from their sin of idolatry."[11]

5. What are the most important elements in the description of the Babylonians (Chaldeans) as given in 1:6-11?

_____

_____

A feared and dreaded people (1:7). "If God's
people refuse to fear him, they will ultimately
be compelled to fear those less worthy of fear."[12]

Earthen ramps (1:10). "Siege ramps built by
attackers to gain access to a fortified city's
walls."[13]

6. In Habakkuk's response in 1:12-14, what attributes of God does the prophet emphasize?

_____

_____

_____

7. In the portrait of the wicked in 1:15-16, what
does Habakkuk emphasize?

_____

_____

_____

8. What is the significance of Habakkuk's question
in 1:17?

_____

_____

_____

9. Thinking further about 1:12-17, what evidence
do you see of Habakkuk's faith in these verses?

_____

_____

_____

_____

For Further Study:
How does Habakkuk's
understanding of
God, as expressed
in Habakkuk 1:12,
compare with what
he would have
known from these
Old Testament pas-
sages: Genesis 21:33;
Deuteronomy 33:27;
Psalm 90:1-2?

For Further Study:
How does Habakkuk's
further understanding
of God, as expressed
in Habakkuk 1:13,
compare with what
he would have known
from these Old
Testament passages:
Deuteronomy 32:4;
Psalm 5:5; 18:26.

For Thought and Discussion:
Is it improper for believers today to question what God is doing in world events? Is it better to just quietly accept whatever we see is happening?

10. Summarize the prophet's situation and attitude as you see these expressed in Habakkuk 2:1.

_____

_____

_____

On the ramparts (2:1). "Habakkuk's 'watch' is evidently portrayed as being on the city walls. . . . On such defenses as these . . . Habakkuk saw himself on duty. . . . His 'ramparts' and 'watch' were the place of responsibility assigned to him, to stand in the council of the Lord and to see his word—a role discharged in attentive, reverent prayer by the same conscientious watchfulness and persistence demanded of the literal watchman."[14]

11. In Habakkuk 2:2-3, as the Lord begins to respond once more to Habakkuk, what does He first ask the prophet to do, and why?

_____

_____

_____

_____

Revelation (2:2). Or "vision" (ESV, NASB, NKJV). This word "commonly refers to the prophetic message from God (see 1 Chronicles 17:15; Proverbs 29:18). . . . The content may be the entire book of Habakkuk, or some shorter portion."[15]

Write down . . . and make it plain (2:2). "Like the Lord's revelation to Moses, this prophecy has a lasting relevance and is to be guarded accordingly."[16]

Awaits an appointed time (2:3). "The following message deals with the fall of Babylon in 539 B.C., about 66 years after Habakkuk's prophecy."[17]

12. What significance do you see in the Lord's statement in 2:4?

_____

_____

_____

Faithfulness (2:4). The Hebrew word "implies fairness, stability, certainty, permanence. . . . In the present context, this quality of reliability and stability is predicated of the 'righteous.' . . . It signifies that his commitment to righteousness is genuine and steadfast."[19]

---

13. What is the Lord emphasizing in the description recorded in 2:5?

_____

_____

_____

14. Summarize the thrust and emphasis in each of the "woe" statements in these sections of chapter 2:

2:6-8

_____

_____

_____

2:9-11

_____

_____

_____

2:12-14

_____

For Further Study: "The key phrase 'but the righteous will live by his faith' summarizes the path of life God sets for his people and is quoted three times in the New Testament, each time highlighting a different aspect of the phrase's meaning."[18] Notice how these words from the final line of Habakkuk 2:4 are quoted by Paul in Romans 1:17 and Galatians 3:11; observe also the fuller quotation in Hebrews 10:38. As you examine the context of each of these New Testament passages, how does this quotation help to clarify the meaning of the gospel?

Optional Application: Reflect on the Lord's words in Habakkuk 2:4. For you personally, what is the meaning of this *righteousness*, this *faith*, and this *life* that are all mentioned here?

For Thought and Discussion: To what extent do any of the descriptions in the "woe" sections of chapter 2 (verses 6-19) reflect the attitudes and attributes of your own nation, or any prominent nation in the world today?

For Further Study: How do the "woes" in Habakkuk 2:6-19 compare with what you observe in the following "woe" passages: Isaiah 5:8-23; Matthew 23:13-32; Luke 6:24-26?

2:15-17

_____

_____

_____

2:18-19

_____

_____

_____

15. What is the special significance of the Lord's statement in 2:14?

_____

_____

_____

The earth will be filled with the knowledge of the glory of the Lord (2:14). "That this may be the case, the kingdom of the world, which is hostile to the Lord and His glory, must be destroyed. This promise therefore involves a threat directed against the Chaldean. His usurped glory shall be destroyed, that the glory of Jehovah . . . of the God of the universe, may fill the whole earth."[20] "The Lord's presence in His temple affirms His Lordship over history and assures us that in the end, His legitimate claim to the whole world will be universally acknowledged."[21]

As the waters cover the sea (2:14). "A figure denoting overflowing abundance."[22]

---

16. What is the special significance of the statement in 2:20?

32

_____

_____

_____

The LORD is in his holy temple; let all the earth be silent before him (2:20). These words may represent the prophet's own conclusion to the oracle he recorded here in chapter 2. "His conclusion in 2:20 may be as much of a self-criticism as it is a statement of the holiness of God."[23]

17. In Habakkuk 1–2, what would you select as the key verse or passage—one that best captures or reflects the dynamics of what these chapters are all about?

_____

_____

_____

18. What do these chapters in Habakkuk communicate most to you about the heart and character of God?

_____

_____

_____

_____

19. List any lingering questions you have about Habakkuk 1–2.

_____

_____

_____

_____

Optional Application: What personal hope and expectation do you gain from the Lord's words in Habakkuk 2:14?

For Further Study: How does the message of Habakkuk 2:14 compare with what you see in Isaiah 45:20-25 and 1 Corinthians 15:24-28, especially in regard to humanity's acknowledgment of God?

For Further Study: What reinforcing links do you see between Habakkuk 2:20 and the following passages: Psalm 11:4; 46:10; Zephaniah 1:7; Zechariah 2:13; Ephesians 2:19-22?

Optional Application: Reflect further on the final verse of Habakkuk 2. What kind of silence before the Lord is appropriate for you at this time?

For Thought and Discussion: Would you say that your own view of history's direction for the future is essentially positive or essentially negative? And how do you think Habakkuk would answer that question?

For the group

You may want to focus your discussion for lesson 2 especially on some of the following issues, themes, and concepts (which are recognized as major overall themes in Habakkuk). Which of these are dealt with in some way in chapters 1–2, and how are they further developed there?

- God's power and sovereignty
- God's justice
- God's goodness and trustworthiness
- God's mercy
- Submission to God's sovereign purpose
- Faith
- God's judgment against humanity's sin

The following numbered questions in lesson 2 may stimulate your best and most helpful discussion: 2, 4, 9, 16, 17, 18, and 19.

Look also at the questions in the margins under the heading "For Thought and Discussion."

1. Leland Ryken and Philip Graham Ryken, eds., *The Literary Study Bible* (Wheaton, IL: Crossway, 2007), introduction to Habakkuk, "The book at a glance."
2. *New Geneva Study Bible* (Nashville: Thomas Nelson, 1995), introduction to Habakkuk, "Characteristics and Themes."
3. Carl E. Armerding, "Habakkuk," in *Daniel and the Minor Prophets*, The Expositor's Bible Commentary, vol. 7, ed. Frank E. Gabaelein (Grand Rapids, MI: Zondervan, 1985), 493.
4. Armerding, 495.
5. *The Complete Word Study Old Testament*, ed. Warren Baker (Chattanooga, TN: AMG, 1994), introduction to Habakkuk.
6. *ESV Study Bible* (Wheaton, IL: Crossway, 2008), at Habakkuk 1:1.
7. Armerding, 494.
8. Armerding, 500.
9. *NIV Study Bible* (Grand Rapids, MI: Zondervan, 1985), at Habakkuk 1:2.
10. Armerding, 502.
11. *Complete Word Study Old Testament*, at Habakkuk 1:5.
12. Armerding, 503.
13. *New Geneva Study Bible*, at Habakkuk 1:10.
14. Armerding, 509.
15. *ESV Study Bible*, at Habakkuk 2:2.

16. Armerding, 511.
17. *NIV Study Bible*, at Habakkuk 2:3.
18. *ESV Study Bible*, introduction to Habakkuk, "Key Themes."
19. Armerding, 513.
20. C. F. Keil and F. Delitzsch, *Commentary on the Old Testament: The Minor Prophets*, vol. 10 (Edinburgh, UK: Clark, 1871; Peabody, MA: Hendrickson, 1996), 410.
21. *New Geneva Study Bible*, introduction to Habakkuk, "Characteristics and Themes."
22. Keil and Delitzsch, 410.
23. *Complete Word Study Old Testament*, at Habakkuk 1:12–2:4.

HABAKKUK 3

Prayer of Faith

Habakkuk's prayer in chapter 3 displays "remarkable power and enigmatic intensity"; these verses "draw on the entire spectrum of salvation history, from Creation and Exodus to the final revelation of God's rule and judgment still awaiting its fulfillment."[1]

1. What would you say is the essence of the prophet's request in Habakkuk 3:2?

_____

_____

_____

For Thought and Discussion: In the opening words of Habakkuk's prayer in this chapter, he speaks of his longing for God to "renew" His "deeds" in the prophet's own day. What "deeds" of the Lord do you most want to see renewed in our day?

The prophet (3:1). See 1:1. This reference "marks a new section, distinct from chapters 1 and 2."[2]

Shigionoth (3:1). This term, which elsewhere in Scripture is used only in Psalm 7:1, "may refer to an instrument or a type of psalm."[3]

In our day, in our time (3:2). Identical phrases in Hebrew; "in the midst of the years . . . in the midst of the years" (ESV, NASB, NKJV). "The repetition . . . is expressive of the earnest longing with which the congregation of the Lord looks for the tribulation to end."[4]

Optional Application: To what extent do you see the prophet's words in Habakkuk 3:2 as a model for your own prayers?

For Further Study: In Habakkuk's psalm (chapter 3), how would you compare verses 3 and 4 with what you see in the words of the blessing from Moses in Deuteronomy 33:2?

2. What is the significance of the phrases in 3:3?

_____

_____

_____

God (3:3). The Hebrew for God's name here can be transliterated as "Eloah" — "a form of the name *Elohim* which occurs only in poetry in the earlier Hebrew writings, which we find for the first time in Deuteronomy 32:15, where it is used of God as the Creator of Israel."[5]

Teman (3:3). "Means 'southland.' God is pictured as coming from the area south of Judah during the exodus."[6]

Mount Paran (3:3). See Numbers 13:3,26; Deuteronomy 33:2.

3. What is being described in 3:4-7, and what is the significance of this?

_____

_____

_____

_____

Plague . . . pestilence (3:5). These terms "refer particularly to the plagues that devastated Egypt (Exodus 9:3,15; Psalm 78:50) and which attended Israel's disobedience to the covenant given at Sinai (Exodus 5:3; Leviticus 26:25; Numbers 14:12; Deuteronomy 28:21; 32:24.)"[7]

Mountains . . . hills (3:6). These are "symbols of grandeur, permanence, and security in the 'earth'; yet they too are revealed as frail and impermanent. Before God's might they are shattered and prostrated."[8]

4. What do you perceive as the best answer to the questions in 3:8?

_____

_____

_____

_____

For Further Study:
How would you compare what you see in Habakkuk 3:6 with Micah 1:4 and Nahum 1:5? What special importance do you see in this imagery?

Rivers . . . streams (3:8). It is "likely" that "the word 'rivers' is equivalent to 'sea': the noun admits the meaning 'currents,' 'watermass,' and is not restricted to inland rivers."[9]

---

5. What is being described in 3:9-13?

_____

_____

_____

_____

As in Psalm 77, the lines in Habakkuk 3:10 "portray the deliverance at the Red Sea as a reenactment of the Flood, itself a reversal and renewal of Creation when the Lord brought life and order out of the waters of the deep. . . . It is this awe-inspiring power of God, the Creator and Judge of all the earth, that is manifested in retribution and salvation at the Red Sea. As at the Cross, a universal cataclysm is compressed into a single, localized event in Israel's history; as at the Cross, that event is destined to shake the universe."[10]

Sun and moon stood still (3:11). "A reference to Joshua's victory at Gibeah (Joshua 10:12-13)."[11]

You came out (3:13). "In the past the Lord came out of His sanctuary for the salvation of His people in distress. This is what Habakkuk expects Him to do again."[12]

6. What is being described in 3:14-15?

_____

_____

_____

The sea . . . horses . . . great waters (3:15). "Verse
15 reverts again to the language of verse 8,
thereby defining verses 8-15 as a unit and
establishing the historical context of the inter-
vening verses; the phrase 'great waters' represents a further allusion to the Exodus from
Egypt."[13]

7. How would you explain and characterize
Habakkuk's response in 3:16?

_____

_____

_____

_____

My heart pounded (3:16). Or, "my body trembles"
(ESV); "my inward parts trembled" (NASB).
"Although trembling on account of the
approaching trouble, the prophet will neverthe-
less exult in the prospect of the salvation that
he foresees (3:18)."[14]

8. a. Summarize Habakkuk's thoughts and convictions as expressed in 3:17-18.

_____

_____

_____

_____

b. What factors do you think influenced the development of these conclusions in Habakkuk's mind and heart?

_____

_____

_____

Fig tree . . . grapes . . . olive crop . . . fields . . . sheep . . . cattle (3:17). "The nouns used in this verse represent the bases of Israel's agricultural economy."[15]

9. How does 3:19 indicate Habakkuk's faith?

_____

_____

_____

For the director of music . . . stringed instruments (3:19). "This kind of liturgical notation suggests that Habakkuk meant this to be a 'prayer' (Habakkuk 3:1) that the faithful would sing together."[16]

10. In your own words, how would you contrast the state of Habakkuk's mind and heart in chapter 3 with what we saw of him in chapter 1?

_____

_____

_____

11. In Habakkuk 3, what would you select as the key verse or passage—one that best captures or reflects the dynamics of what this chapter is all about?

For Thought and Discussion: In light of events and developments in today's uncertain world, what is the value and appropriateness of the kind of attitudes evidenced by the prophet in Habakkuk 1:17-18?

Optional Application: Reflect again on the prophet's words in Habakkuk 3:16-19. What elements here could also serve as valid and genuine expressions of your own faith?

For Further Study: How would you compare the thoughts in Habakkuk 3 with the themes found in the following Old Testament chapters: Deuteronomy 33; Exodus 15; Psalm 17; 18; 68; 77; 90?

_____

_____

_____

"The prophet's response of faith in the third chapter demonstrates that for him the power and goodness of God have been satisfactorily reconciled with the evil and suffering that he sees in the world."[17]

12. What does this last chapter in Habakkuk communicate most to you about the heart and character of God?

_____

_____

_____

13. List any lingering questions you have about Habakkuk 3.

_____

_____

_____

Reviewing the book of Habakkuk

14. What have you learned most or appreciated most in your study of the book of Habakkuk?

_____

_____

_____

15. Recall again the words of Isaiah 55:10-11, where God reminds us that in the same way He sends rain and snow from the sky to water the earth and nurture life, so also He sends His words to accomplish specific purposes. What would you suggest are God's primary purposes for the message of Habakkuk in the lives of His people today?

_____

_____

_____

_____

Optional Application: Which verses in the book of Habakkuk would be most helpful for you to memorize, so you have them always available in your mind and heart for the Holy Spirit to use?

16. Review again the guidelines given for our thought-life in Philippians 4:8 — "Whatever is true, whatever is noble, whatever is right, whatever is pure, whatever is lovely, whatever is admirable — if anything is excellent or praiseworthy — think about such things." As you reflect on all you've read in the book of Habakkuk, what stands out to you as being particularly *true*, or *noble*, or *right*, or *pure*, or *lovely*, or *admirable*, or *excellent*, or *praiseworthy* — and therefore well worth thinking more about?

_____

_____

_____

_____

_____

17. Because all of Scripture testifies ultimately of Christ, where does *Jesus* come most in focus for you in this book?

_____

_____

_____

_____

18. In your understanding, what are the strongest ways in which Habakkuk points us to humanity's need for Jesus and for what He accomplished in His death and resurrection?

_____

_____

_____

_____

19. Recall again Paul's words in Romans 15:4, reminding us that the Old Testament Scriptures can give us endurance and perseverance on one hand, as well as comfort and encouragement on the other. In your own life, how do you see the book of Habakkuk living up to Paul's description? In what ways does it help to meet your personal needs for both *perseverance* and *encouragement*?

_____

_____

_____

_____

For the group

You may want to focus your discussion for lesson 3 especially on some of the following issues, themes, and concepts (which are recognized as major overall themes in Habakkuk). Which of these are dealt with in some way in chapter 3, and how are they further developed there?

- God's power and sovereignty
- God's justice
- God's goodness and trustworthiness
- God's mercy
- Submission to God's sovereign purpose
- Faith
- God's judgment against humanity's sin

The following numbered questions in lesson 3

44

may stimulate your best and most helpful discussion: 8, 10, 11, 12, 13, 14, 15, 16, 17, 18, and 19.

Remember to look also at the "For Thought and Discussion" questions in the margins.

1. Carl E. Armerding, "Habakkuk," in *Daniel and the Minor Prophets*, The Expositor's Bible Commentary, vol. 7, ed. Frank E. Gabaelein (Grand Rapids, MI: Zondervan, 1985), 520.
2. Armerding, 523.
3. *ESV Study Bible* (Wheaton, IL: Crossway, 2008), at Habakkuk 3:1.
4. C. F. Keil and F. Delitzsch, *The Minor Prophets*, Commentary on the Old Testament, vol. 10 (Edinburgh, UK: Clark, 1871; Peabody, MA: Hendrickson, 1996), 416.
5. Keil and Delitzsch, 417.
6. *NIV Study Bible* (Grand Rapids, MI: Zondervan, 1985), at Habakkuk 3:3.
7. Armerding, 526.
8. Armerding, 527.
9. Armerding, 527–528.
10. Armerding, 529.
11. *ESV Study Bible*, at Habakkuk 3:11.
12. *New Geneva Study Bible* (Nashville: Thomas Nelson, 1995), at Habakkuk 3:13.
13. Armerding, 532.
14. Keil and Delitzsch, 428.
15. Armerding, 533.
16. *ESV Study Bible*, at Habakkuk 3:19.
17. Leland Ryken and Philip Graham Ryken, eds., *The Literary Study Bible* (Wheaton, IL: Crossway, 2007), introduction to Habakkuk, "The book at a glance."

ZEPHANIAH 1–2

Day of Judgment

"There is a compelling simplicity about Zephaniah's message: he has only one topic, and he never digresses from it"; this prophecy represents "a structured treatise on the theme of 'the day of the Lord.'"[1]

"The purpose of this prophetic book is to predict the coming judgment of God against Judah and against surrounding pagan nations, with a complementary vision of God's restoration of a remnant of his people at the end of the book."[2]

"Zephaniah is a book of vivid contrasts. Compared to other prophets, he paints a darker picture of God's judgment, and a brighter picture of Israel's future glory. The extreme contrast reflects the divided religious loyalties of the people of Judah."[3]

"In a sense, the history of the times has nothing to say about Zephaniah's

Optional Application: After His resurrection, when Jesus was explaining Old Testament passages to His disciples, we read that He "opened their minds so they could understand the Scriptures" (Luke 24:45). Ask God to do that kind of work in *your* mind as you study the book of Zephaniah so you're released and free to learn everything here He wants you to learn—and so you can become as bold and worshipful and faithful as those early disciples of Jesus. Express this desire to Him in prayer.

For Thought and Discussion: How familiar is the book of Zephaniah to you? What have been your previous impressions of this book?

message. Throughout the book there is a sense of distance from historical events. . . . Zephaniah is rooted in the flow of history, but his concern is only with the goal . . . the day when calamitous human efforts to run the world will coincide in an awesome climax with the Lord's purposes of judgment and hope."[4]

"Zephaniah prophesied in the southern kingdom of Judah when Josiah (640–609 B.C.) was king. . . . Zephaniah would have been a contemporary of Jeremiah, whose call came in Josiah's thirteenth year (627 B.C.)."[5]

1. Think again of Jeremiah 23:29, where God says His Word is "like fire" and "like a hammer." He can use the Scriptures to burn away unclean thoughts and desires in our hearts. He can also use Scripture, with hammer-like hardness, to crush and crumble our spiritual hardness. From your study of Zephaniah, how do you most want to see the fire-and-hammer power of God's Word at work in your own life? Again, express this longing in a written prayer to God.

   _____

   _____

   _____

   _____

2. Glance ahead through the pages of Zephaniah and briefly scan all three chapters. What are your overall impressions of the book, including its structure and its themes?

   _____

   _____

For Further Study:
For more background on King Josiah (mentioned in Zephaniah 1:1), see 2 Kings 22–23 and 2 Chronicles 34–35.

———————————————

———————————————

3. Now turn your focus to the first chapter of Zephaniah. What do you know already about the kings mentioned in Zephaniah 1:1?

———————————————

———————————————

———————————————

During the reign of Josiah (1:1). 640–609 BC. "Zephaniah lived to see the corrupt kings Manasseh and Amon replaced by a good king, Josiah. Yet he knew that things had already gone beyond the point where a change of government would change the destiny of the world. And even though he lived to see Josiah's reform sweep the country, he did not revise his message."[6]

4. As concerning the entire world, what does the Lord promise to do in Zephaniah 1:2-3?

———————————————

———————————————

———————————————

The wicked (1:3). "The reason why everything is under judgment remains constant throughout time: the wicked. This word, even more commonplace in Hebrew than in English, indicates humankind's ordinary 'badness,' which constitutes the greatest environmental threat of all. Even now the earth is in ruins. Everything of beauty and joy (including the whole animal creation) is diseased by contagion from sinful humans (Genesis 3:16-19). . . . Sin has also infected our moral perceptions: we are not—nor can we be—trustworthy judges of what is fitting."[7]

5. As concerning His people, what does the Lord promise to do in 1:4-6, and why?

_____

_____

_____

_____

Baal (1:4). "Baal was the god of productivity: his function in Canaanite religion was to make land, animals, and humans fertile. Baal was another name for the gross national product, and wherever people see bank balances, prosperity, a sound economy, productivity, and mounting exports as the essence of their security, Baal is still worshiped. Baal was also the god of religious excitement (1 Kings 18:26b) and sexual free-for-all (Numbers 25:1-3). Human sexual acts were publicly offered to him to prompt him to perform his work of fertilization. . . . Wherever excitement in religion becomes an end in itself and wherever the cult of 'what helps' replaces joy in 'what's true,' Baal is worshiped."[8]

The day of the LORD is near (1:7). See also 1:14-16; 3:8,9-11,16,19-20. "The distinctive feature of the book of Zephaniah is that this vision of judgment is couched in the motif of a coming 'day of the LORD.' As the variations on this theme accumulate, it becomes evident that there is a specific and immediate day of the Lord coming for Judah but also intermediate days of the Lord that will occur later in history, as well as an ultimate, eschatological day of the Lord that will occur at the end of human history."[9]

---

6. What are the most important distinctives of "the day of the LORD" as revealed in the following sections of this opening chapter in Zephaniah?

50

1:7-9

_____

_____

_____

1:10-11

_____

_____

_____

1:12-13

_____

_____

_____

1:14-16

_____

_____

_____

1:17-18

_____

_____

_____

The officials and the king's sons (1:8). "Leaders carry a burden of responsibility inseparable from their position. It matters how they live, what they do, how they legislate. . . . And this applies equally to leaders in the church."[10]

The temple of their gods (1:9). Or "their master's house" (ESV), or "their Lord's house" (ESV margin). "A reference to Yahweh. In relation to the religious leaders of his day . . . Zephaniah lays a specific charge: they practice ritual and give

For Further Study:
As you reflect on
the meaning of "the
day of the LORD" in
Zechariah, compare
and review other
prophecies con-
cerning this theme
in Isaiah 2:12-21;
13:6-13; Jeremiah
46:10; Ezekiel 7:10-14;
Joel 1:15; 2:1,11,31;
3:14; Amos 5:18-20;
8:9-10; Obadiah 15;
Malachi 4:5.

For Further Study:
In the New
Testament, what
additional under-
standing of "the
day of the LORD"
do we find in
2 Thessalonians 1:8-9
and 2 Peter 3:7-13?

teaching and direction at variance with the
word of God. . . . Worship must conform to the
will of God as its unerring standard."[11]

7. In light of all that is revealed in 1:7-18, what
   do you see as the particular significance of the
   command in 1:7?

_____

_____

_____

_____

_____

The LORD will do nothing, either good or bad
(1:12). "This is not atheism as a dogma but
practical atheism; it does not say, 'God is
not there,' but, 'God is not here'—not that
God does not exist but that he does not
matter."[12]

The great day of the LORD is near (1:14). "There
is a God to whom the human race will one day
have to give an account, however marginal
they may seek to make him in the present. . . .
The day of the Lord is not arbitrary; it is the
logical outgrowth of what humankind is, it
will bring what humankind deserves, and it
will expose the uselessness of what humans
trust."[13]

The Warrior (1:14). "The Warrior here is best
understood as the Lord himself."[14]

Bitter (1:14). "Knowing the Lord as Scripture
reveals him, the bitterness of his cry is both
that of outraged holiness and that of an
anguished heart."[15]

Because they have sinned against the LORD
(1:17). "To Zephaniah (see James 2:10-11) the
mere fact of sin excited and merited the whole
weight of divine rage."[16]

8. As their response to these revelations in chapter 1, what does the Lord request His people to do in Zephaniah 2:1-3?

_____

_____

_____

Gather yourselves together, you shameful nation (2:1). "This gathering represents the concerted effort of the nation to heed the prophet's warning. Zephaniah is concerned more with national repentance than with the repentance of only a small sector within the nation."[17]

Seek the Lord (2:3). "Typical of Scripture, the first move is to go directly to the Lord. Every other religion says, Become righteous, become humble; then perhaps God will accept you. But in the Bible the only way to flee *from* God is to flee *to* him. . . . It must be done in a spirit of humility ('humble ones') with the intention of obedience ('determined to do as he decides')."[18]

9. As concerning the Philistines, what future does the Lord promise in 2:4-7?

_____

_____

_____

"The second section of Zephaniah's book [2:4—3:8] . . . describes how judgment will cover all the earth, justifies this divine action by making specific accusations, and qualifies judgment by an unexpected and unexplained note of hope (2:11; 3:8). From the vantage point of Judah, the prophet looks west to

For Further Study:
How do you see the message of Zephaniah 2:3 reinforced and expanded in 1 Peter 1:17-19 and Philippians 2:12-13?

Optional Application: In God's eyes, are you a true "seeker"? Reflect on the words of Zephaniah 2:3; what urgency and relevance do these commands have in *your* life at this time? (See also Matthew 6:33.)

53

Philistia, east to Moab/Ammon, south to
Cush, and north to Assyria, finally bring-
ing the dire message home to Judah."[19]

The word of the Lᴏʀᴅ is against you (2:5). "The
word of the Lord is the central, determinative
factor in the course of history."[20]

The remnant (2:7). This concept represents a
"key element of Zechariah's teaching (2:7,9;
3:13). . . . It is interesting that the meaning of Zephaniah's name, 'the Lᴏʀᴅ hides,' is
so closely associated with this aspect of his
prophecy."[21] "The fact remains: in a world
brought to ruin under divine judgment, the
Lord is at work on behalf of his people, to
preserve, enrich, and bring them into the
possession of what he has promised."[22]

---

10. As concerning the peoples of Moab and
    Ammon, what future does the Lord promise in
    2:8-11?

    _____

    _____

    _____

***The insults of Moab and the taunts of the
Ammonites*** (2:8). Ammon and Moab "had
often threatened to occupy Israelite territory."[23]
Both these nations "descended from Lot
through his incestuous relationship with his
daughters (Genesis 19:30-38)."[24]

***Nations will bow down to him, all of them in their
own lands*** (2:11). "Zephaniah offers his own
comment on verse 11 in 3:9-11."[25]

---

11. As concerning the Cushites, what future does
    the Lord promise in 2:12?

_____

_____

_____

12. As concerning the Assyrians, what future does the Lord promise in 2:13-15?

_____

_____

_____

For Further Study:
What do you learn about the hostility of Moab and Ammon toward Israel in Amos 1:13-15 and 2:1-3?

Leaving Nineveh utterly desolate (2:13). "The city of Nineveh fell approximately twenty years after this prophecy was given."[26]

13. What do chapters 1 and 2 of Zephaniah reveal most about the Lord's power and sovereignty?

_____

_____

_____

14. What do these chapters reveal most about the Lord's loving care for His people?

_____

_____

_____

15. What do these chapters reveal most about the Lord's righteousness and holiness?

_____

_____

_____

16. In Zephaniah 1–2, what would you select as the key verse or passage — one that best captures or reflects the dynamics of what these chapters are all about?

_____

_____

_____

17. List any lingering questions you have about Zephaniah 1–2.

_____

_____

_____

_____

For the group

You may want to focus your discussion for lesson 4 especially on some of the following issues, themes, and concepts (which are recognized as major overall themes in Zephaniah). Which of these are dealt with in some way in chapters 1–2, and how are they further developed there?

- The "day of the LORD"
- God's wrath and judgment against sin
- Repentance
- Redemption
- God's salvation and restoration for His people
- The kingdom of God

The following numbered questions in lesson 4 may stimulate your best and most helpful discussion: 2, 7, 13, 14, 15, 16, and 17.

Look also at the questions in the margins under the heading "For Thought and Discussion."

1. J. Alec Motyer, "Zephaniah," in *The Minor Prophets*, ed. Thomas Edward McComiskey (Grand Rapids, MI: Baker, 2009), 897, 899.
2. Leland Ryken and Philip Graham Ryken, eds., *The Literary Study Bible* (Wheaton, IL: Crossway, 2007), introduction to

Zephaniah, "The book at a glance."

3. *The Complete Word Study Old Testament*, ed. Warren Baker (Chattanooga, TN: AMG, 1994), introduction to Zephaniah.
4. Motyer, 899.
5. *New Geneva Study Bible* (Nashville: Thomas Nelson, 1995), introduction to Zephaniah, "Date and Occasion."
6. Motyer, 911.
7. Motyer, 911.
8. Motyer, 912.
9. Ryken and Ryken, introduction to Zephaniah, "The book at a glance."
10. Motyer, 919.
11. Motyer, 919–920.
12. Motyer, 921.
13. Motyer, 922–923.
14. Motyer, 923.
15. Motyer, 923.
16. Motyer, 924.
17. Motyer, 926.
18. Motyer, 927.
19. Motyer, 931.
20. Motyer, 931.
21. *Complete Word Study Old Testament*, introduction to Zephaniah.
22. Motyer, 933.
23. *NIV Study Bible* (Grand Rapids, MI: Zondervan, 1985), at Zephaniah 2:8.
24. *ESV Study Bible* (Wheaton, IL: Crossway, 2008), at Zephaniah 2:8.
25. Motyer, 935.
26. *Complete Word Study Old Testament*, at Zephaniah 2:13.

ZEPHANIAH 3

Day of Hope

"The certainty of God's favor to those who trust in him for salvation climaxes the book [of Zephaniah] and brings it to conclusion."[1]

1. Express in your own words the reasons given for the warning in Zephaniah 3:1-2.

   _____

   _____

   _____

   _____

The city (3:1). Jerusalem. "The city Zephaniah accuses has heard divine revelation (3:2a), has known the divine law (3:2b), and has been invited to trust (3:2c) and approach God (3:2d). It has a familiar civil and religious structure: princes, judges, prophets, priests (3:3-4). It is the city that the Lord indwells (3:5) — their own Zion!"[2]

2. What faults on the part of the leaders of God's people are exposed in 3:3-4?

   _____

**For Thought and
Discussion:** Review
the leadership fail-
ings exposed in
Zephaniah 3:3-4.
Does this relate in any
way to leaders among
God's people today?

3. Compare how the Lord is described in 3:5 with
   how the leaders are described in 3:3-5. What
   contrasts are emphasized here?

4. What does 3:6-7 reveal most about God's mind
   and heart?

5. What command does the Lord give in 3:8, and
   what reason does He give?

6. Express in your own words the future that is
   envisioned in 3:9-10.

Then I will purify the lips of the peoples (3:9). Or,
"For at that time I will change the speech of the
peoples to a pure speech" (ESV); "For then I will
restore to the peoples a pure language" (NKJV).

60

"The 'purified speech' of 3:9 identifies 3:9-10 as the reversal of Babel (Genesis 11:1-9). . . . Just as the central motivation of Babel was to organize life without God, so now the unified world centralizes the Lord, using its newfound speech to call on the name of the Lord. . . . Zephaniah tells nothing of the means whereby this will be done, only that divine action has remedied the cause and the effect of Babel."[3]

Shoulder to shoulder (3:9). Literally, "with one shoulder" ("with one accord," ESV, NKJV).

Cush (3:10). Ethiopia. "Cush is singled out as an instance of the whole world worshiping the Lord."[4]

7. How would you personally express the future that's envisioned in 3:11?

\
\
\
\

8. What characteristics of the Lord's true people are emphasized in 3:12-13?

\
\
\
\

9. What are the people told to do in 3:14-15, and for what reason?

\
\
\
\

For Further Study:
In Zephaniah 3:12-13, reflect further on God's promises concerning a preserved remnant of His people. How does this compare with what you see in these passages: Isaiah 8:9-22; Micah 2:12; 5:8; 7:18?

For Further Study:
In the future envisioned for the true remnant of God's people, Zephaniah writes, "They will eat and lie down and no one will make them afraid" (3:13). How is this pastoral imagery seen further in the following passages: Psalm 23:1; 74:1; 77:20; 80:1; 95:7; Isaiah 40:11; 63:11; Ezekiel 34:12-23; 36:37; Matthew 25:33; John 10:14-16; 21:16; Hebrews 13:20; 1 Peter 2:25?

The Lord has taken away your punishment (3:15).
Or, "The Lord has taken away the judgments
against you" (ESV). Here the Lord is particularly
shown to be "the satisfied God who found a way
to 'set aside the judgments' that stood against
his people. Isaiah (45:21) expressed the same
thought by describing him as 'a righteous God
and a Savior,' and Paul echoed it by writing
of one who is 'just and the justifier' (Romans
3:26, KJV). It is one thing to deal with sin within
the sinner so that conscience no longer accuses
(Zephaniah 3:11): this is the guiltiness of sin.
It is a different thing to deal with sin as it
outrages the holy character of God: this is the
offense of sin, and it constitutes a deeper and
more necessary work, for there can be no salvation until God is satisfied."[5]

The Lord . . . is with you (3:15). "This indwelling
is the objective verification of his inward satis-
faction over his people. There is nothing now
to alienate the Holy One. . . . This indwelling is
also the central divine objective in the work of
redemption (Exodus 29:46)."[6]

10. What are the people told to do in 3:16-17, and
for what reason?

_____

_____

_____

_____

In his love he will no longer rebuke you (3:17).
Or, "He will be quiet in His love" (NASB).
"Silence in His love is an expression used to
denote love deeply felt, which is absorbed in its
object with thoughtfulness and admiration."[7]

His love (3:17). "Most often the Lord's love is
expressed by the Hebrew word *hesed*. This is
the love that issues in commitment, the 'ever-
unfailing' fidelity of love, love that lives in the
will as much as in the heart. Here, however,

the word is *'ahābâ*, the passionate love of Jacob for Rachel (Genesis 29:20) and of Michal for David (1 Samuel 18:28), the fond love of Jacob for Joseph (Genesis 37:3), Uzziah's devotion to gardening (2 Chronicles 26:10), Jonathan's deep friendship with David (1 Samuel 18:3), the devotee's delight in the Lord's law (Psalm 119:97). This too is the Lord's love for his people, a love that delights him, makes him contemplate his beloved with wordless adoration, a love that cannot be contained but bursts into elated singing."[8]

11. What future for God's people is envisioned in 3:18-19?

_____

_____

_____

12. What do you see as the special significance of the promise in 3:20?

_____

_____

_____

_____

"Before your very eyes," says the LORD (3:20). "'Before your very eyes' assures the Lord's people that they will actually and certainly enter into and enjoy this promise for themselves; and 'says the LORD' underwrites the promise with a specified pledge. It is something to which the Lord has made his personal commitment."[10]

13. In Zephaniah 3, what would you select as the key verse or passage—one that best captures or reflects the dynamics of what this chapter is all about?

_____

Optional Application: Reflect deeply on God's promises to His people in Zephaniah 3:17-20. "In a world of turmoil and persecution, God reveals His presence, power, and protection."[9] What further appreciation of God, and what personal encouragement do you find in these verses for this time in your life?

_____

_____

_____

14. What does this last chapter in Zephaniah communicate most to you about the heart and character of God?

_____

_____

_____

_____

15. List any lingering questions you have about Zephaniah 3.

_____

_____

_____

_____

Reviewing the book of Zephaniah

16. In your study of the book of Zephaniah, what have you learned most and appreciated most?

_____

_____

_____

17. What have you learned in this book about the biblical concept of "the day of the LORD"?

_____

_____

_____

_____

18. Recall again the message of Isaiah 55:10-11—in the same way God sends rain and snow from the sky to water the earth and nurture life, so also He sends His words to accomplish specific purposes. What would you suggest are God's primary purposes for the message of Zephaniah in the lives of His people today?

_____

_____

_____

_____

19. Review again the guidelines in Philippians 4:8—"Whatever is true, whatever is noble, whatever is right, whatever is pure, whatever is lovely, whatever is admirable—if anything is excellent or praiseworthy—think about such things." As you reflect on all you've read in the book of Zephaniah, what stands out to you as being particularly *true,* or *noble,* or *right,* or *pure,* or *lovely,* or *admirable,* or *excellent,* or *praiseworthy*—and therefore well worth thinking more about?

_____

_____

_____

_____

20. Because all of Scripture testifies ultimately of Christ, where does *Jesus* come most in focus for you in this book?

_____

_____

_____

_____

21. In your understanding, what are the strongest ways in which Zephaniah points us to humanity's need for Jesus and for what He accomplished in His death and resurrection?

_____

_____

_____

_____

22. Recall again Paul's reminder in Romans 15:4
that the Old Testament Scriptures can give
us endurance and perseverance, as well as
comfort and encouragement. In your own life,
how do you see the book of Zephaniah living
up to Paul's description? In what ways do the
Scriptures help to meet your personal needs for
both *perseverance* and *encouragement*?

_____

_____

_____

_____

For the group

You may want to focus your discussion for lesson 5
especially on some of the following issues, themes,
and concepts (which are recognized as major overall themes in Zephaniah). Which of these are dealt
with in some way in chapter 3, and how are they
further developed there?

- The "day of the LORD"
- God's wrath and judgment against sin
- Repentance
- Redemption
- God's salvation and restoration for His people
- The kingdom of God

The following numbered questions in lesson 5
may stimulate your best and most helpful discussion: 12, 13, 14, 15, 16, 17, 18, 19, 20, 21, and 22.

Remember to look also at the "For Thought and
Discussion" questions in the margins.

1. Leland Ryken and Philip Graham Ryken, eds., *The Literary
Study Bible* (Wheaton, IL: Crossway, 2007), introduction to

Zephaniah, "The book at a glance."

2. J. Alec Motyer, "Zephaniah," in *The Minor Prophets*, ed. Thomas Edward McComiskey (Grand Rapids, MI: Baker, 2009), 941.
3. Motyer, 951–952.
4. Motyer, 952.
5. Motyer, 956–957.
6. Motyer, 957.
7. C. F. Keil and F. Delitzsch, *Commentary on the Old Testament: The Minor Prophets*, vol. 10 (Edinburgh, UK: Clark, 1871; Peabody, MA: Hendrickson, 1996), 461.
8. Motyer, 958.
9. *The Complete Word Study Old Testament*, ed. Warren Baker (Chattanooga, TN: AMG, 1994), at Zephaniah 3:17-19.
10. Motyer, 962.

HAGGAI

The Lord's House and the People's Hope

"Haggai is the first of the prophets who spoke to the exiles after they had returned to Palestine. . . . Haggai ministered in 520 B.C. between the months of August and December. He delivered four messages during this time. . . .

"His ministry had a single focus: urging God's people to be obedient, especially in the rebuilding of the temple. . . .

"Following Haggai's ministry, work on the temple was begun again, and completed in 516 B.C. It is not known whether Haggai lived to see its completion."[1]

In this brief book we see Haggai "as a man of conviction. He has the unique place among the prophets of having been really listened to and his words obeyed. The people did what he preached, and in a mere four years the temple was complete. Though his words were plain and not poetic, he had one major point to make; and he made it forcefully and well."[2]

Optional Application: After His resurrection, when Jesus was explaining Old Testament passages to His disciples, we read that He "opened their minds so they could understand the Scriptures" (Luke 24:45). Ask God to do that kind of work in *your* mind as you study the book of Haggai, so you're released and free to learn everything here He wants you to learn — and so you can become as bold and worshipful and faithful as those early disciples of Jesus. Express this desire to Him in prayer.

For Thought and Discussion: How familiar is the book of Haggai to you? What have been your previous impressions of this book?

1. Remember again Jeremiah 23:29, where God says His Word is "like fire" and "like a hammer" — burning away unclean thoughts and desires in our hearts, as well as crushing and crumbling our spiritual hardness. From your study of Haggai, how do you most want to see the fire-and-hammer power of God's Word at work in your own life? Again, express this longing in a written prayer to God.

_____

_____

_____

_____

2. Glance ahead through the pages of Haggai and briefly scan both chapters. What are your overall impressions of the book, including its structure and its themes?

_____

_____

_____

_____

3. Now turn your focus to the first chapter of Haggai. What are the main points being communicated in the prophetic words spoken in Haggai 1:1-6, and what is their significance?

_____

_____

_____

_____

In the second year of King Darius, on the first day of the sixth month (1:1). August 29, 520 BC.[3]

To Zerubbabel (1:1). "Because Zerubbabel was the ruler in charge of the nation at the time (see

70

Ezra 1–6 for the details), the book is addressed to Zerubbabel instead of to the nation."[4]

The Lord Almighty (1:2). Or, "the Lord of hosts" (ESV, NASB, NKJV). "The divine name *Yahweh* (the Lord) occurs thirty-four times in the thirty-eight verses of this book, and fourteen of these stress divine omnipotence with the ancient epithet *Lord of hosts*."[5] "One gets the distinct impression from these two chapters that Haggai was speaking the very word of God with all possible authority and unction."[6]

The Lord's house (1:2). In a "long tradition . . . the prophets linked the messianic day to the house concept. . . . Haggai also lived within this tradition. The presence of the Lord in his house among his people was a pledge of the great day and the greater coming and presence."[7]

For Further Study: Regarding the importance (from God's perspective) of His temple, the house of the Lord, and its connection with the promised Messiah — what further insight do you gain from the following passages: 2 Samuel 7; Isaiah 4:2-6; 62:8-9; Malachi 3:1-4?

"After the decree of the Persian emperor Cyrus in 538 B.C., exiles led by Zerubbabel returned to the land of Judah (Ezra 1). At the site of Solomon's temple they built an altar and . . . also prepared to rebuild the temple, but work stopped in response to opposition from neighboring enemies. In the sixteen years that followed, the people built themselves houses, but no work was done on the Lord's house until the prophets Haggai and Zechariah rebuked and challenged the people (Ezra 4:24–5:2)."[8]

"In Old Testament thought, the house [God's tabernacle or temple] was not desired for itself, as a sort of lucky charm. . . . The house was the outward form of the real presence of the Lord among his people. To refuse to build the

71

house was at best saying that it did not matter whether the Lord was present with them. . . . Not to build the house was not to want the Lord as and for himself."[9]

Give careful thought to your ways. . . . Give careful thought to your ways (1:5,7). "To set the heart upon one's ways . . . to consider one's conduct, and lay it to heart . . . your designs and actions, and their consequences."[10]

Never have enough . . . never have your fill . . . are not warm (1:6). "Haggai does not say any went hungry, thirsty, or naked, but that they had fallen short of what they wanted. . . . This was the problem: they had goods but the good life eluded them; they were not hungry but neither were they satisfied; they were dressed but they were not comfortable."[11]

In a purse with holes in it (1:6). "It was not that they had no money; it was that the money did not go far."[12]

---

4. From what you see in 1:7-11, what does the Lord want the people to better understand?

_____

_____

_____

_____

5. How would you summarize the problem being defined in Haggai 1:1-11, and how did it arise?

_____

_____

_____

_____

"To leave the house unbuilt was just another way of saying, 'It matters not whether God is with us. When we get living conditions and the economy right and develop a decent standard of living and negotiate proper wage rates — then we will have time for religion and for God.'"[14]

6. How did Haggai's hearers respond, according to 1:12?

_____

_____

_____

The whole remnant of the people (1:12,14). "Once they respond to the Lord's word, they show themselves to be truly the returned community — not just those who have come back to the land but those who have come back to the Lord in repentance."[15]

And the people feared the LORD (1:12). This remnant was "returning to him in obedience . . . with a reverence so deep that it merited description as their being afraid of the Lord. Even to this extent were their hearts new."[16]

7. What is the significance of Haggai's further prophetic words in 1:13?

_____

_____

_____

The LORD's messenger, gave this message of the LORD to the people (1:13). Haggai is described

For Further Study:
How would you compare the message of Haggai 1:1-11 with what you see in Amos 4:6-11? How are these passages alike, and what perspectives do they share?

Optional Application:
"Haggai's scriptural worldview taught him that the forces of nature are but agents in the hands of God. He is the power to be reckoned with in the practical affairs of life and the organizing power behind the scenes. . . . The vital question for us is whether we share his worldview. Do we believe that economic facts are divine appointments? We who live in an affluent society plagued with dissatisfaction . . . do we share Haggai's insistence on an immediacy of the presence and action of the living God?"[13] How would you answer these questions? To what extent do you share Haggai's worldview?

For Further Study:
As you reflect on the Lord's call to His people in Haggai 1:1-11 to rebuild the temple, what links do you see with the words of Jesus in Matthew 6:33 regarding our calling to God's kingdom and righteousness?

Optional Application: Perhaps the words of the prophet Haggai in 1:13 are words that *you* need to hear at this time. If so, what is the personal significance of those words?

here in this way "to reflect the new popular awareness of him and his message that began to emerge in 1:12."[17]

I am with you (1:13). "The Hebrew words are different from 'Immanuel,' but their message is the same. Without God we can do nothing; with him all things are possible."[18]

8. a. What do we learn in 1:14-15 about the response of the people and their rulers?

_____

_____

_____

_____

   b. What do you see as the most significant elements in this response?

_____

_____

_____

"When we begin to respond to the word of God (1:12), he immediately uses his word for our further encouragement (1:13) and follows with a renewing, inward work in our spirits to mobilize us for obedience (1:14). The word of God is his chosen instrument of renewal, in which the key human factor is obedience and the key divine factor an energizing work of God making that obedience possible."[19]

The twenty-fourth day of the sixth month (1:15). September 21, 520 BC.

"The Lord knows the needs of his people and through the prophet Haggai tackles the problem of depression and despondency head on. Believers today need the same word of encouragement because of the often shattered state of the church, the seeming fruitlessness of effort, and the slow progress in building the temple of the Holy Spirit in fellowship and in personal life (1 Corinthians 3:16; 6:19)."[20]

9. Describe the situation found in Haggai 2:1-3.

_____

_____

_____

The twenty-first day of the seventh month (2:1). October 17, 520 BC.

Like nothing (2:3). "Haggai was a sound psychologist: the first step in ministry to the despondent is to admit with them the reality of what is causing the despondency. The new house was indeed 'absolutely nothing' by comparison! But, having identified with them, he can now turn to the positive steps necessary as a corrective."[21]

10. What encouragement and counsel does the Lord offer the people and their leaders in 2:4-5?

_____

_____

_____

For Further Study:
Reflect further on
the Lord's encour-
aging "I am with
you" statements in
Haggai 1:13 and 2:4.
How is the message
of this encourage-
ment enriched
and deepened in
the following pas-
sages: Genesis 26:3;
Exodus 3:12; Numbers
14:9; Isaiah 41:10;
43:2; Jeremiah 1:8;
Matthew 28:20;
Acts 18:9-10?

**Optional
Application:** Reflect
deeply on the Lord's
repeated command
to the leaders as well
as to all the people in
Haggai 2:4-5. What is
the encouragement
the Lord wants
now to communi-
cate through these
words to you and to
the people in your
church?

The Lᴏʀᴅ Almighty (2:4). Or, "the Lᴏʀᴅ of hosts"
(ESV, NASB, NKJV). Also in verses 6, 7, 8, 9, and
11. "God, throughout this passage, is called
the 'Lᴏʀᴅ of hosts' (which literally means 'Lord
of armies'). What a comforting name for the
people of Israel, who felt that they were a tiny
powerless province of Persia!"[22] "The key to
tackling despondency is found here: stop listening to ourselves and start listening to him and
his word of promise."[23]

But now be strong. . . . Be strong . . . and work
(2:4). "The problem was essentially one of attitude.
So the primary command was to take courage.
When the people did that, the command to
'work' would be fulfilled quite naturally."[24]

For I am with you (2:4). "The most uplifting thing
they or anyone could hear was that God was
with them."[25]

*This is what I covenanted with you when you
came out of Egypt* (2:5). "By Haggai's day,
centuries had passed since that great covenant-
ing, and in that passage of time Israel had been
guilty of every known sin, unfaithfulness, dis-
trust, disloyalty, neglect, and betrayal of their
God. But human sin and frailty cannot over-
throw God's faithfulness (Romans 3:3). The
promise still stood."[26]

11. What promises from God are stated in 2:6-9,
    and what is their significance?

    _____

    _____

    _____

    _____

Once more shake the heavens and the earth
(2:6). "The first 'shaking' took place at Mount
Sinai, when God gave the law to Moses (Exodus
19:16); the second shaking will come at the end
of the world."[27]

***In a little while I will . . . shake the heavens
and the earth, the sea and the dry land***
(2:6). "An announcement of the coming day
of God's judgment on the nations—which the
fall of Persia to Alexander the Great (333–330
B.C.) would foreshadow."[28] "As is common
in the prophets, the near and distant future
are telescoped, or compressed together. Here
references to the glory of the second temple are
juxtaposed with a picture of the final universal
judgment on the cosmos. While this shaking
may be prefigured by political events occurring
shortly after the time of Haggai, the ultimate
shaking of the created order is still to come."[29]
See also verses 21-22 of this chapter.

Desired (2:7). Or "treasures" (ESV); "wealth" (NASB).
"Though the Hebrew term . . . could refer to
a person (i.e., the Messiah), the immediate
context here favors a reference to the things
desired by all nations (i.e., the things precious
to them). Verse 8 speaks of such precious
things, and the decree of King Darius, during whose reign Haggai ministered, alludes
to precious things being contributed to the
temple building project (Ezra 6:3-5,8-9). Here
Haggai probably echoes Isaiah's promise of an
Israel made rich by the wealth of the nations
(Isaiah 60:5). In other words, he speaks of the
Messianic age."[30]

For Further Study:
As you think about
God's promise in
Haggai 2:6 to "once
more shake the
heavens and the
earth," how is the
meaning of this
promise clarified in
Hebrews 12:25-29?

**For Thought and
Discussion:** Why is
encouragement so
valuable? And why do
we need it so often?

12. In Haggai 2:1-9, how are the people encouraged
and rewarded in their obedience to the Lord?

_____

_____

_____

_____

In this place I will grant peace (2:9). "The original purpose of the temple as a work of peace
will be realized."[31]

For Further Study:
How is the promise
of peace in Haggai
2:9 given further sub-
stance in these pas-
sages: Psalm 85:8-9;
Isaiah 9:6-7; 57:18-21;
Luke 2:14; John
20:19-21; Acts 10:36;
Ephesians 2:14-17;
Colossians 1:19-20?

"In essence Haggai returns here [in 2:10-19]
to the foundational message of 1:1-11. The
difference is not one of content but of
emphasis. In 1:1-11 he concerned himself
mainly with diagnosis of the malady and
how it could be cured; here he repeats
himself but goes on to the promise of the
healthy and fulfilled life that awaits the
cured patient."[32]

13. What are the priests being made aware of in
    their dialogue with Haggai in 2:10-14?

_____

_____

_____

"If he [Haggai] said to us, 'If you touch
something with a dirty hand you will
leave a dirty mark but if you touch something with a clean hand you will not leave
a clean mark,' we could only agree. . . .
Things like sacrificial meats could become
holy. . . . But, like the clean hand that does
not leave a clean mark, this holy status
was not communicable."[33]

"In short, holiness is not catching"; in 2:10-14,
Haggai "wished to show the people that it
is easier to fall into sin than it is to fall into
righteousness."[34]

The twenty-fourth day of the ninth month (2:10).
December 18, 520 BC.

---

14. From what you see in 2:15-19, what does the
Lord want His people to better understand?

_____

_____

_____

_____

Yet you did not return to me (2:17). "Failure in
crops and failure in devotion belong together.
The heart of their problem was that they acted
as if life could be run without reference to God
and as if grace would be theirs even though
they neglected the means of grace. It would
hardly be stretching the meaning of 2:17b to
paraphrase: 'But you did not want me!' At this
point the coldness of the human heart and the
hurt in the divine heart meet."[35]

15. To summarize 2:10-19, how would you describe
and explain the future blessing promised to
God's people, and the particular way in which
He makes this promise?

_____

_____

_____

_____

From this day on I will bless you (2:19). "God's
grace overcomes the sin and defilement of
His people. Though He chastises them, in the
end mercy triumphs over judgment."[36] "He is
asserting a matter of pure spiritual essence: the
first call to the people of God is to love the Lord
their God with all their heart and to do all that
he requires, whereby he will live at peace in
their midst. This is the key to blessing." [37]

79

16. In the final vision in this book (see Haggai 2:20-23), what does God promise?

_____

_____

_____

_____

17. What messianic dimension do you see in the words of 2:20-23?

_____

_____

_____

_____

Zerubbabel governor of Judah (2:21). "Zerubbabel, the Davidic descendant, was in reality the heir to nothing. There was no throne for him to mount or crown to wear, no empire to rule or royal acclaim to enjoy. It is not even certain that his title of governor was anything more than honorific. The whole Davidic enterprise had long since run into the sand. But to write off the Davidic promises would be to forget the faithfulness of God, who does not lie or change his mind (Numbers 23:19)."[38]

Like my signet ring (2:23). "A kind of seal that functioned as a signature. . . . Like other seals it could be used as a pledge or guarantee of full payment."[39] "It symbolizes the possession and enjoyment of a close and precious relationship."[40] "Like a king sealing legal documents with his ring, the Lord will set his authentic impression upon the world through his royal representative. Zerubbabel, a descendant of one previously discarded (Jeremiah 22:24-27), is the ring placed back on the hand of the divine King. God's promise to bless his people and the whole world through the house of David still stands (see Matthew 1:1)."[41]

"The Book of Haggai, which began on such a discouraging and depressing note, ends on an uplifting and promising one. Haggai's first message was one of indictment; his last one is of a great and blessed future for the people of God. As we now know, that future was much further away than either Haggai or Zerubbabel thought. But in the mind of God, it is as close and certain as tomorrow's rising sun." [42]

18. What have you learned most or appreciated most in your study of the book of Haggai?

_____

_____

_____

_____

19. What would you select as the key verse or passage in Haggai—one that best captures or reflects the dynamics of what this book is all about?

_____

_____

_____

20. What does the book of Haggai communicate most to you about the heart and character of God?

_____

_____

_____

_____

Optional
Application: Which
verse or verses in the
book of Haggai would
be most helpful for
you to memorize so
you have them always
available in your mind
and heart for the Holy
Spirit to use?

21. List any lingering questions you have about the
book of Haggai.

_____

_____

_____

_____

22. Because all of Scripture testifies ultimately of
Christ, where does *Jesus* come most in focus for
you in this book?

_____

_____

_____

_____

23. Again, recall Paul's reminder in Romans
15:4 — the Old Testament Scriptures can
give us endurance and perseverance as well
as comfort and encouragement. In your own
life, how do you see the book of Haggai living
up to Paul's description? In what ways do the
Scriptures help to meet your personal needs for
both *perseverance* and *encouragement*?

_____

_____

_____

_____

For the group

You may want to focus your discussion for lesson
6 especially on the following issues, themes, and
concepts, which are recognized as major overall
themes in Haggai. How do you see these being dealt
with in this book?

• The temple of God and the worship of God
• The triumph of God's kingdom over evil

- God's sovereignty
- Holiness
- Industriousness
- Encouragement
- Hope and anticipation
- Longing

The following numbered questions in lesson 6 may stimulate your best and most helpful discussion: 2, 15, 18, 19, 20, and 21.
Look also at the questions in the margins under the heading "For Thought and Discussion."

1. *The Complete Word Study Old Testament*, ed. Warren Baker (Chattanooga, TN: AMG, 1994), introduction to Haggai.
2. Robert L. Alden, "Haggai," in *Daniel and the Minor Prophets*, The Expositor's Bible Commentary, vol. 7, ed. Frank E. Gabaelein (Grand Rapids, MI: Zondervan, 1985), 572.
3. As reckoned by Joyce G. Baldwin in *Haggai, Zechariah, Malachi: An Introduction and Commentary* (Downers Grove, IL: InterVarsity, 1972), 29, and cited in J. Alec Motyer, "Haggai," in *The Minor Prophets*, ed. Thomas Edward McComiskey (Grand Rapids, MI: Baker, 2009), 967. So also for the dates given at Haggai 1:15; 2:1; 2:10.
4. Leland Ryken and Philip Graham Ryken, eds., *The Literary Study Bible* (Wheaton, IL: Crossway, 2007), introduction to Haggai, "The book at a glance."
5. Motyer, 964.
6. Alden, 579.
7. Motyer, 965–966.
8. Motyer, 966.
9. Motyer, 974.
10. C. F. Keil and F. Delitzsch, *Commentary on the Old Testament: The Minor Prophets*, vol. 10 (Edinburgh, UK: Clark, 1871; Peabody, MA: Hendrickson, 1996), 476.
11. Motyer, 977.
12. Motyer, 977.
13. Motyer, 978.
14. Motyer, 979.
15. Motyer, 981.
16. Motyer, 981.
17. Motyer, 982.
18. Alden, 583.
19. Motyer, 981.
20. Motyer, 987.
21. Motyer, 987.
22. *Complete Word Study Old Testament*, at Haggai 2:6-9.

23. Motyer, 987.
24. Alden, 585.
25. Alden, 585.
26. Motyer, 988.
27. Alden, 586.
28. *NIV Study Bible* (Grand Rapids, MI: Zondervan, 1985), at Haggai 2:6.
29. *New Geneva Study Bible* (Nashville: Thomas Nelson, 1995), at Haggai 2:6.
30. *New Geneva Study Bible*, at Haggai 2:7.
31. Motyer, 989.
32. Motyer, 994.
33. Alden, 996.
34. Alden, 588.
35. Motyer, 997.
36. *New Geneva Study Bible*, at Haggai 2:19.
37. Motyer, 998.
38. Motyer, 1001–1002.
39. *NIV Study Bible*, at Haggai 2:23.
40. Motyer, 1002.
41. *ESV Study Bible* (Wheaton, IL: Crossway, 2008), at Haggai 2:23.
42. Alden, 591.

ZECHARIAH 1–4
Visions in the Night

"In terms of length and complexity, the prophecy of Zechariah is the major book among what the ancient Hebrew rabbis called The Twelve (the minor prophets). The original audience of the book was (as with the book of Haggai) the remnant who had returned from Babylonian exile. Because of its visionary and symbolic modes and its futuristic orientation, the book of Zechariah (along with the book of Daniel) is often considered to be the Old Testament parallel to the New Testament book of Revelation."[1]

"The ministry of Zechariah, which began in 520 B.C., overlapped that of Haggai but continued long after Haggai ceased to prophesy. The meaning of Zechariah's name, 'the LORD remembers,' is also the theme of the book. . . .

"Zechariah, like Haggai, had a ministry of encouragement. There is one fundamental difference between their

Optional Application: After His resurrection, when Jesus was explaining Old Testament passages to His disciples, we read that He "opened their minds so they could understand the Scriptures" (Luke 24:45). Ask God to do that kind of work in *your* mind as you study the book of Zechariah, so you're released and free to learn everything here He wants you to learn—and so you can become as bold and worshipful and faithful as those early disciples of Jesus. Express this desire to Him in prayer.

For Thought and Discussion: How familiar is the book of Zechariah to you? What have been your previous impressions of this book?

messages in that Haggai, after challenging the people to proceed with the rebuilding of the temple, focused primarily on God's immediate presence and the blessings that were at hand, with only brief references to ultimate glory. With Zechariah, the proportions are reversed. His encouragement was related to the ultimate glorification of Israel through the coming of the Messiah."[2]

1. Recall again Jeremiah 23:29, where God says His Word is "like fire" and "like a hammer"— burning away unclean thoughts and desires in our hearts, as well as crushing and crumbling our spiritual hardness. From your study of Zechariah, how do you most want to see the fire-and-hammer power of God's Word at work in your own life? Again, express this longing in a written prayer to God.

_____

_____

_____

_____

2. Glance ahead through the pages of Zechariah and briefly scan each chapter. What are your overall impressions of the book, including its structure and its themes?

_____

_____

_____

_____

3. Now turn your focus to the first chapter of this book. In Zechariah 1:2-6, what fault does the Lord find with His people, and what exactly does He ask the current generation to do about it?

_____

_____

_____

_____

For Thought and Discussion: As you reflect on the broad warning expressed to God's people in Zechariah 1:2-6, how do you think this relates to God's people today?

In the eighth month of the second year of Darius (1:1). October/November 520 BC.[3]

The first six chapters of Zechariah record eight visions that the prophet saw during a single night. These visions "embody in symbolic form what God plans to do. This part of the book needs to be approached as we approach the New Testament book of Revelation, that is, by first allowing the images and symbols to activate our imagination and then exploring what those details symbolize."[4]

"The first six chapters are filled with references to the temple and the reinstitution of worship there. In other ways, too, these visions send a message of encouragement to the exiles and their leaders that God is present with them as they start life over in Jerusalem. But as we read we are continuously aware that the imagery, motifs, and vocabulary reach out beyond the immediate situation to (a) the Messiah and the salvation that he brought with his redeeming death and resurrection, and also to (b) end-times prophecies."[5]

4. On this night of visions (chapters 1–6 in Zechariah), describe and summarize

what Zechariah sees and hears in the first vision
(1:7-17).

_____

_____

_____

_____

The twenty-fourth day of the eleventh month
(1:7). February 15, 519 BC.

5. How does your imagination respond to what
   you read in 1:7-17? What impressions and questions arise?

_____

_____

_____

_____

6. How do verses 14, 16, and 17 in chapter 1 shed
   light on the meaning and significance of this
   first vision?

_____

_____

_____

_____

7. In the second of the prophet's visions this night,
   describe what he sees and hears, as recorded in
   1:18-21.

_____

_____

_____

_____

8. How does your imagination respond to what you read in 1:18-21?

_____

_____

_____

_____

9. How does 1:21 shed light on the meaning and significance of this second vision?

_____

_____

_____

10. In the third of the prophet's visions, summarize what he sees and hears, as recorded in chapter 2.

_____

_____

_____

_____

11. How does your imagination respond to what you read in chapter 2?

_____

_____

_____

_____

12. How does Zechariah 2:3-5 shed light on the meaning and significance of this third vision?

_____

_____

_____

_____

13. As the fourth of Zechariah's visions unfolds this night, summarize what this man Joshua sees, hears, and experiences, as Zechariah records it in chapter 3.

_____

_____

_____

_____

14. How does your imagination respond to what you read in chapter 3?

_____

_____

_____

_____

Joshua the high priest (3:1). "While the high priest had great authority throughout much of Israel's history, the absence of a reigning monarch in the postexilic period appears to have lifted the high priest to even greater prominence, especially in matters relating to the temple."[6] Joshua here "represents the sinful nation of Israel (see verses 8-9)."[7]

Satan (3:1). The name means "Accuser." "The text does not require us to assume that this figure is Satan; he may function only as a symbol of an accuser, a role endemic to any legal disputation."[8]

Angel of the Lord (3:1). "In all probability, the angel of the Lord represents Yahweh as the judge in this court scene, for it is the angel who carries out the implications of Yahweh's rebuke in verse 2 by removing the nation's guile (verse 4) and speaking on Yahweh's behalf (verse 7)."[9]

Joshua was dressed in filthy clothes (3:3). "We expect to see him clothed in white vestments with the ephod on his chest, but we

90

are shocked at what we see. His garments are soiled with filth, and the description of his condition repulses us. . . . Must not God turn his back on this repulsive sight and vent his anger at this affront to his holiness? It seems that the accuser is justified in calling for God's judgment on the sin this filth represents."[10]

15. What particular importance do you see in the instructions given to Joshua in 3:6-7?

_____

_____

_____

_____

For Further Study: Reflect on the cleansing and reclothing of Joshua as you see it in Zechariah 3:3-5. How does the message of this passage link with New Testament teaching in Romans 8:30 and 2 Corinthians 3:18?

For Further Study: How does the message of Zechariah 3:6-7 compare with God's instructions to His people in Exodus 19:5?

The angel of the LORD gave this charge to Joshua (3:6). "Because Joshua represents the people, the assurances are in reality directed to them. . . . The reality that the rich apparel symbolizes — the restoration of the nation's glory — is conditioned on national obedience."[11]

---

16. How does Zechariah 3:8-10 shed light on the meaning and significance of this fourth vision?

_____

_____

_____

_____

My servant, the Branch (3:8). These are messianic titles. "Except for the prophecy of Isaiah, Zechariah is the most messianic prophetic book of the Old Testament."[12] See also Zechariah 6:12.

The stone (3:9). "In all probability, this stone is a finishing stone (a capstone or cornerstone)

91

whose inscription Yahweh is already carving
and the placement of which would mark the
completion of the structure. . . . The stone
symbolizes a greater temple whose ministra-
tions effect the removal of guilt—the temple
of the Branch (6:12) over which God intently
watched."[13]

Seven eyes (3:9). "Perhaps symbolic of infinite
intelligence (omniscience)."[14] "Yahweh's eyes
are watching over the building efforts (the
stone). . . . God is watching the building efforts
intently and will see them through to completion."[15] Look ahead also to the final sentence in
4:10.

Under your vine and fig tree (3:10). "A proverbial
picture of peace, security, and contentment."[16]

17. In the fifth of the prophet's visions this night,
    describe what Zechariah sees and hears, as
    recorded in chapter 4.

    _____

    _____

    _____

    _____

18. How does your imagination respond to what
    you read in chapter 4?

    _____

    _____

    _____

    _____

The angel . . . returned and woke me up (4:1).
"We cannot fully understand what occurred;
we only know that he again became aware of
the mysterious presence of the mediating angel
arousing him to prepare for another vision (see
Jeremiah 31:26)."[17]

92

Lampstand with a bowl (4:2). "The vision here was probably of seven lamps arranged around a large bowl that served as a bountiful reservoir of oil. . . . The bowl represents an abundant supply of oil, symbolizing the fullness of God's power through his Spirit."[18]

Seven lamps . . . seven channels to the lamps (4:2). The repeated number "represents the abundant light shining from the lamps (seven being the number of fullness or completeness)."[19]

19. Look closely at the exchange recorded in 4:4-6. What is the particular significance of the angel's answer?

_____

_____

_____

By my Spirit (4:6). "The continual supply of oil to the reservoir [4:2,12] symbolizes God's supply of what the people needed to complete the building of the temple. . . . If the oil represents the divine energy that moved the work to completion, the lamps must then represent in some way the work on the temple building and, beyond that, God's glorious kingdom. His words will not fail, nor his promises prove empty. By his active presence among his people, he sustains them, in spite of forces that oppose his kingdom."[20]

20. What is being emphasized in the prophetic words of 4:7-10?

_____

_____

_____

_____

Mighty mountain (4:7). "The great mountain
before Zerubbabel is to become a plain, not by
human power, but by the Spirit of the Lord
[4:6]. . . . The great mountain . . . is apparently
a figure denoting the colossal difficulties which
rose up mountain-high at the continuation and
completion of the building of the temple."[21]

God bless it! God bless it! (4:7). Or, "Grace, grace
to it!" (ESV, NASB, NKJV). "The people attribute the
work to God. . . . They do not celebrate their
own abilities or national might, for they had
little of that. The people learned of the mighty
power of the Holy Spirit at their disposal."[22]

The day of small things (4:10). "The greatest of
efforts and institutions all have had small
beginnings. The church began with a handful
of timorous disciples, and now its domain is the
world."[23]

The seven (4:10). See 3:9.

21. Review the exchange recorded in 4:11-14; what
is the significance of the angel's answer?

_____

_____

_____

Pour out golden oil (4:12). "We are to picture the
oil flowing in profusion, not simply dripping
from the spouts. This element of the vision
underscores the abundant supply of God's
Spirit for the task at hand."[24] "Oil, regarded
according to its capacity to invigorate the body
and increase the energy of the vital spirits, is
used in the Scriptures as a symbol of the Spirit
of God . . . at work in the world and indwelling
the church."[25]

Two who are anointed (4:14). Literally, "two sons
of oil." The two are perhaps Joshua and Zerubbabel. These two men "stood out from the
community as these branches [4:12] did from

94

the trees, and as 'sons of oil' they sustained a relationship to the enabling power of God."[26]

22. In Zechariah 1–4, what would you select as the key verse or passage—one that best captures or reflects the dynamics of what these chapters are all about?

_____

_____

_____

23. What do these chapters in Zechariah communicate most to you about the heart and character of God?

_____

_____

_____

_____

24. List any lingering questions you have about Zechariah 1–4.

_____

_____

_____

_____

For the group

You may want to focus your discussion for lesson 7 especially on some of the following issues, themes, and concepts (which are recognized as major overall themes in Zechariah). Which of these are dealt with in some way in chapters 1–4, and how are they further developed there?

• The coming Messiah
• Judgment from God
• Salvation

95

- Blessing from God
- Events of the future and of the end times
- The promised Messiah
- Holiness

The following numbered questions in lesson 7 may stimulate your best and most helpful discussion: 2, 5, 11, 14, 18, 22, 23, and 24.

Remember to look also at the "For Thought and Discussion" questions in the margins.

1. Leland Ryken and Philip Graham Ryken, eds., *The Literary Study Bible* (Wheaton, IL: Crossway, 2007), introduction to Zechariah, "The book at a glance."
2. *The Complete Word Study Old Testament*, ed. Warren Baker (Chattanooga, TN: AMG, 1994), introduction to Zechariah.
3. *ESV Study Bible* (Wheaton, IL: Crossway, 2008), chart, "Dates of the Oracles in Zechariah," at Zechariah 1:10-11. So also for the date given here at Zechariah 1:7.
4. Ryken and Ryken, introduction to Zechariah, "The book at a glance."
5. Ryken and Ryken, introduction to Zechariah, "Time frame of the visions."
6. Thomas Edward McComiskey, "Zechariah," in *The Minor Prophets* (Grand Rapids, MI: Baker, 2009), 1069.
7. *NIV Study Bible* (Grand Rapids, MI: Zondervan, 1985), at Zechariah 3:1.
8. McComiskey, 1069.
9. McComiskey, 1069.
10. McComiskey, 1070.
11. McComiskey, 1073–1074.
12. Ryken and Ryken, introduction to Zechariah, "The book at a glance."
13. McComiskey, "Zechariah," 1079.
14. *NIV Study Bible*, at Zechariah 3:9.
15. McComiskey, 1079.
16. *NIV Study Bible*, at Zechariah 3:10.
17. McComiskey, 1082.
18. *NIV Study Bible*, at Zechariah 4:2.
19. *NIV Study Bible*, at Zechariah 4:2.
20. McComiskey, 1085–1086.
21. C. F. Keil and F. Delitzsch, *Commentary on the Old Testament: The Minor Prophets*, vol. 10 (Edinburgh, UK: Clark, 1871; Peabody, MA: Hendrickson, 1996), 536–537.
22. McComiskey, 1088.
23. McComiskey, 1089.
24. McComiskey, 1092.
25. Keil and Delitzsch, 534–535.
26. McComiskey, 1093.

ZECHARIAH 5–8

More Visions and Encouragement

Chapters 5 and 6 continue narrating the series of eight visions that the prophet Zechariah experienced on a single night; while chapters 7 and 8 focus on repentance and promised blessing for God's people.

For Thought and Discussion: What do you think it would be like to personally experience the kind of visions from God that Zechariah writes about?

1. In the sixth of Zechariah's visions on this night (recall 1:8), describe what he sees and hears, as recorded in Zechariah 5:1-4.

   _____

   _____

   _____

   _____

2. How does your imagination respond to what you read in 5:1-4? What impressions and questions arise?

   _____

   _____

   _____

   _____

3. How does 5:3 shed light on the meaning and significance of this sixth vision?

_____

_____

_____

4. In the seventh of the prophet's visions, describe what Zechariah sees and hears, as recorded in 5:5-11.

_____

_____

_____

_____

Babylonia (5:11). Or, "Shinar" (ESV, NASB, NKJV). "'Shinar' is an old name for Babylon, which normally represented evil."[1]

---

5. How does your imagination respond to what you read in 5:5-11?

_____

_____

_____

_____

6. How does 5:8-9 shed light on the meaning and significance of this seventh vision?

_____

_____

_____

Chariots . . . horses (6:1-2). Zechariah's eight visions on this night "are organized so that the first (1:7-17) and last (6:1-8) correspond to one another in the imagery of horses and chariots."[2] The interpretation of these chariots in chapter 6 is given in verse 5. "The 'chariots' in this passage symbolize God's power directed earthward for the purpose of judgment (see Psalm 68:17; Isaiah 66:15)."[3]

7. In Zechariah's final vision this night, summarize what he sees and hears, as recorded in 6:1-8.

_____

_____

_____

_____

8. How does your imagination respond to what you read in 6:1-8?

_____

_____

_____

_____

9. How would you summarize the meaning and significance of this eighth vision?

_____

_____

_____

_____

The word of the Lord came to me (6:9). This phrasing introduces a prophetic oracle. (See also 7:4,8; 8:1,18.)

10. Summarize the prophetic message given to Zechariah in 6:9-15.

_____

_____

_____

_____

11. How do the prophetic words in Zechariah 6:11-13 link with what you learned in chapter 3 about the high priest Joshua and about "the Branch"?

_____

_____

_____

The Branch (6:12). "A messianic title, the importance of which explains its occurrence here and in 3:8. Isaiah first used the term to denote the Messiah (Isaiah 4:2). Jeremiah then developed it as a title for the Davidic descendant who would rule on David's throne (Jeremiah 23:5-6; 33:15-16). Zechariah joins the royal and priestly offices in this title. Early Jewish interpreters saw it as a messianic title. All this shows the preparation in the Old Testament for the truth that Christ is our High Priest (Hebrews 4:14; 7:24; 9:11) and our King (Hebrews 1:8; Matthew 22:41-46). He is our Savior and our Lord."[4]

It is he who will build the temple of the LORD, and he will be clothed with majesty and will sit and rule on his throne (6:13). "The emphatic clause that begins this verse draws our attention away from Joshua to the Branch: 'It is not Joshua, it is *he* — the Branch — who will build Yahweh's temple.' Another emphatic statement follows: 'It is *he* — that is, the Branch, not Joshua — who will bear royal honor.'"[5]

Those who are far away (6:15). Recall the promise in 2:11 concerning "many nations" who "will

100

be joined with the LORD." "We reflect the full-orbed theology of Zechariah when we view 'those who are far off' [6:15] as Gentiles who join in the building of the kingdom of God."[7]

Help to build the temple of the LORD (6:15).
"Not the Second Temple [erected by the exiles returning from Babylon], but the kingdom of God over which the Branch rules."[8]

This will happen if you diligently obey the LORD your God (6:15). "God's blessings come only to the godly remnant. The union of believing Gentiles with unrepentant Jews is unthinkable. The prophet here establishes that the Lord can work only through a godly remnant."[9]

"Zechariah was interested in the spiritual renewal of the postexilic community. Here he deals further with this problem. The purpose of chapters 7 and 8 is to impress on the people their need to live righteously in response to their past judgment and future glory."[10]

12. How would you summarize the messages of judgment given to God's people in 7:1-7, and why they were given?

_____

_____

_____

_____

In the fourth year of King Darius . . . on the fourth day of the ninth month (7:1).
December 7, 518 BC.[11]

Should I mourn and fast in the fifth month (7:3).
"The fifth month was the month in which the

For Further Study: The messianic prophecy in Zechariah 6:13 portrays "a priest on his throne." "The messianic Branch will combine the two offices of king and priest in full accord."[6] How does the New Testament affirm the union of these two offices in Christ, in these passages: 1 Timothy 6:15; Hebrews 1:3; 8:1; Revelation 19:16?

For Thought and Discussion: Think about the qualities mentioned by the Lord in Zechariah 7:9. In our culture today, how much value is placed upon these things?

For Further Study:
Note the issue of
fasting that arises in
Zechariah 7:3. What
helpful biblical guide-
lines and perspective
concerning this prac-
tice are given in Isaiah
1:11-17 and 58:1-7?

temple in Jerusalem had been destroyed by
Nebuchadnezzar nearly 70 years earlier. Now
that the temple was being rebuilt, it was natural to question whether there was any need
to observe the rite any longer."[12] "The fasts
had been observed in exile, but should they
be continued in these better times back in the
homeland?"[13]

In the fifth and seventh months (7:5). "Zechariah's
ruling . . . also included the fast observed in the
seventh month commemorating the assassina-
tion of Gedaliah (Jeremiah 41:1-3)."[14]

Was it really for me that you fasted? (7:5).
"Though the original inquiry reflected a ritual
concern, the Lord's response asks a deeper
question: 'When you fasted and mourned, was
it really out of a concern over the loss of my
favor? If you stop fasting and return to normal eating and drinking, does that mean an
abandonment of that concern?' If the people
had learned the lesson that the destruction
of the temple was intended to teach, and had
truly repented and turned from their sins, then
they could stop fasting. The temple was being
rebuilt. But if they have simply been fasting for
themselves all along, then their fasting was a
waste of time."[15]

Eating and drinking (7:6). "The prophet's insistent
probing moves from the people's failure to take
God into account in their fasting (verse 5) to a
failure to take him into account when they eat
their meals; that is, they do not consider God
as the provider of their daily bread."[16]

13. What further message of judgment is given in
7:8-14, and on what basis?

_____

_____

_____

_____

14. How would you describe true spirituality from God's perspective as taught in 7:9-10?

_____

_____

_____

_____

___

They refused to pay attention (7:11). This verse offers "a vivid picture of willful refusal to obey God."[17] "The lesson to the Jews of the restoration period is clear: Do not be like your unrepentant, unfaithful, disobedient, covenant-breaking forefathers, or you will suffer a similar fate. One indispensable ingredient in true spirituality is a dogged attentiveness to familiar truths, but they did not 'pay attention.'"[18]

By his Spirit through the earlier prophets (7:12). "The Spirit of God is the manifestation in time of the divine personality, and the prophets, by virtue of their relationship to God's Spirit (Micah 3:8), were agents of his Spirit, communicating God's will."[20]

___

15. How would you summarize the messages of promised blessing given to God's people in 8:1-8?

_____

_____

_____

_____

___

Burning with jealousy (8:2). "Here the divine jealousy is directed toward the restoration of Israel."[21]

Jerusalem will be called the Faithful City (8:3). Or, "the faithful city" (ESV). See also Isaiah 1:26.

Optional Application: To what extent do you see the commands in Zechariah 7:9-10 as instructive and authoritative for your own life? What changes in your lifestyle or behavior might they be calling for from you?

For Further Study: The words of Zechariah 7:8-10 "comprise a collage of prophetic voices that does not appear to contain revelational material original to Zechariah."[19] What similarities do you see between these words of Zechariah and the following passages: Jeremiah 5:28; 7:5-6,25; 21:12; 22:3,15; 26:5; 29:19; 35:15; 44:4; Hosea 4:1; 6:4; 10:12; 12:6; Micah 6:8?

For Further Study: Zechariah specifically acknowledges the Spirit of God's role in speaking through the prophets (see 7:12). How do you see this divine inspiration asserted also in Nehemiah 9:20,30 and 2 Peter 1:21?

For Further Study:
How does the future picture given in Zechariah 8:4-5 compare with what you see in Isaiah 65:20-25?

For Further Study:
In Zechariah 8:8 we see a great covenant promise that God often repeats. What emphasis and implications do you see for this promise in these passages: Genesis 17:7-8; Exodus 6:7; 19:5-6; 29:45-46; Leviticus 11:45; 22:33; 25:38; 26:12,44-45; Numbers 15:41; Deuteronomy 4:20; 29:12-13; Jeremiah 31:33; 32:38; Ezekiel 37:27; 2 Corinthians 6:16; Revelation 21:3?

"Jerusalem did not acquire this character in the period after the captivity, in which, though not defiled by gross idolatry, as in the times before the captivity, it was polluted by other moral abominations no less than it had been before. Jerusalem becomes a faithful city for the first time through the Messiah, and it is through Him that the temple mountain first really becomes the holy mountain."[22]

But will it seem marvelous to me? (8:6). "The implication is that it will not be too difficult for God to accomplish. . . . The word *incredible* . . . captures the basic sense of this root, which describes activity 'beyond normal ability or comprehension' as well as the awe that such activity may inspire. Yahweh of hosts will not regard the promise of Jerusalem's great repopulation as 'incredible' because it is not beyond his power to fulfill it."[23]

From . . . the east and the west (8:7). "The regathering here will be universal."[24]

I will be faithful and righteous to them (8:8). "Israel's restoration depends on the dependable—'faithful and righteous'—God."[25]

16. What further messages of promised blessing are given in 8:9-17?

_____

_____

_____

_____

The prophets . . . who were present (8:9). These included Haggai and Zechariah. (See Ezra 5:1-2; Haggai 1:1; Zechariah 1:1.)

I will give all these things as an inheritance to the remnant of this people (8:12). "Yahweh's blessing on the people must include the spiritual benefits his people enjoy from his hand.

104

These benefits belong to the believer today, multiplied a thousandfold by the guarantees of the new covenant (Jeremiah 31:31-34)."[26]

You will be a blessing (8:13). "In his postresurrection appearance, Christ pictured the benign effect the gospel will have on the nations as it goes forth, beginning at the very city in which Zechariah penned his prophecy (Luke 24:47)."[27]

Sound judgment (8:16). Or, "judgments that . . . make for peace" (ESV). "The root idea of the word seems to be 'wholeness,' 'completeness,' 'soundness,' though it is used principally of a state of 'well-being,' 'health,' 'harmony,' 'peace,' 'security,' and 'prosperity.'"[28]

17. How would you summarize the messages of promised blessing in 8:18-23?

_____

_____

_____

_____

From all languages and nations (8:23). "Revelation 5:9 speaks of the redeemed from 'every tribe and tongue and people and nation.' Salvation then is worldwide, not in the sense that every human being is redeemed, but that the children of God are chosen from every language and ethnic group of the world."[29]

18. In Zechariah 5–8, what would you select as the key verse or passage—one that best captures or reflects the dynamics of what these chapters are all about?

_____

_____

_____

For Further Study: How does the situation described in Zechariah 8:10 compare with the one pictured in Haggai 2:17-19 and Amos 4:6-11?

Optional Application: In Zechariah 8, the repeated call to God's people is this: "Let your hands be strong. . . . Do not be afraid, but let your hands be strong" (8:9,13). In what particular work for God is it time now for *you* to be strong and unafraid?

Optional Application: What call upon your own life and actions do you see in the commands ("These are the things you are to do") given to God's people in Zechariah 8:16-17?

19. What do these chapters in Zechariah communicate most to you about the heart and character of God?

_____

_____

_____

_____

20. List any lingering questions you have about Zechariah 5–8.

_____

_____

_____

_____

For the group

You may want to focus your discussion for lesson 8 especially on some of the following issues, themes, and concepts (which are recognized as major overall themes in Zechariah). Which of these are dealt with in some way in chapters 5–8, and how are they further developed there?

- The coming Messiah
- Judgment from God
- Salvation
- Blessing from God
- Events of the future and of the end times
- The promised Messiah
- Holiness

The following numbered questions in lesson 8 may stimulate your best and most helpful discussion: 2, 5, 8, 14, 15, 16, 17, 18, 19, and 20.

Remember to look also at the "For Thought and Discussion" questions in the margins.

1. *The Complete Word Study Old Testament*, ed. Warren Baker (Chattanooga, TN: AMG, 1994), at Zechariah 5:11.

106

2. *New Geneva Study Bible* (Nashville: Thomas Nelson, 1995), at Zechariah 1:7-17.
3. *Complete Word Study Old Testament*, at Zechariah 6:5.
4. *New Geneva Study Bible*, at Zechariah 6:12.
5. Thomas Edward McComiskey, "Zechariah," in *The Minor Prophets* (Grand Rapids, MI: Baker, 2009), 1116.
6. Kenneth L. Barker, "Zechariah," in *Daniel and the Minor Prophets*, The Expositor's Bible Commentary, vol. 7, ed. Frank E. Gabaelein (Grand Rapids, MI: Zondervan, 1985), 640.
7. McComiskey, 1121.
8. McComiskey, 1121.
9. McComiskey, 1121.
10. Barker, 643.
11. *ESV Study Bible* (Wheaton, IL: Crossway, 2008), chart, "Dates of the Oracles in Zechariah," at Zechariah 1:10-11.
12. *ESV Study Bible*, at Zechariah 7:2-3.
13. Barker, 643.
14. *ESV Study Bible*, at Zechariah 7:5.
15. *ESV Study Bible*, at Zechariah 7:7.
16. McComiskey, 1127.
17. McComiskey, 1132.
18. Barker, 647.
19. McComiskey, 1130.
20. McComiskey, 1132.
21. Barker, 650.
22. C. F. Keil and F. Delitzsch, *The Minor Prophets*, Commentary on the Old Testament, vol. 10 (Edinburgh, UK: Clark, 1871; Peabody, MA: Hendrickson, 1996), 563.
23. McComiskey, 1138–1139.
24. Barker, 651.
25. Barker, 651.
26. McComiskey, 1147.
27. McComiskey, 1148.
28. Barker, 652–653.
29. *New Geneva Study Bible*, at Zechariah 8:23.

ZECHARIAH 9–11

The Coming Messiah and His Rejection

"Part II of the Book of Zechariah [chapters 9–14] contains two undated oracles, though they probably belong to Zechariah's old age (shortly after 480 B.C.)"; here we recognize "the wide scope of the prophecies and the frequent emphasis on the eschaton [end times], particularly the arrival of the great Messianic Era. While chapters 1–8 contain occasional glimpses of future events, chapters 9–14 are almost exclusively eschatological."[1]

1. Proverbs 2:1-5 tells about the sincere person who truly longs for wisdom and understanding, and who searches the Scriptures for it — as if there were treasure buried there. Such a person, this passage says, will come to understand the fear of the Lord and discover the knowledge of God. As you continue exploring the book of Zechariah, what "buried treasure" would you like God to help you find here — to show you what God and His wisdom are really like? If you have this desire, how would you express it in your own words of prayer to God?

2. What are the most important things God promises to do in Zechariah 9:1-8?

_____

_____

_____

_____

A prophecy: The word of the Lord (9:1). Or, "The burden of the word of the Lord" (NASB, NKJV). "The Hebrew for this phrase occurs only two other times in the Old Testament (Zechariah 12:1; Malachi 1:1)."[2] "'Burden' implies that the prophet was under strong compulsion to deliver the message from God."[3]

"There is little doubt that Zechariah's prophecy of the fates of these cities intersects with the course of Alexander's bold military expeditions against Syria-Palestine in 333 B.C."[4]

Hadrak (9:1). "An area in northern Syria that encompassed Damascus and neighboring Hamath (verse 2)."[5]

Damascus (9:1). "The capital of Syria. Known chiefly as a mercantile center, Damascus continued to be the major city of Syria during the Persian period."[6]

The eyes of all people and all the tribes of Israel are on the Lord (9:1). This phrase "may be rendered 'For the eye of the LORD is on all mankind, as well as on the tribes of Israel' (as in NIV margin)."[7] "Yahweh's eye is focused on all humankind as well as on Israel. It leads us to expect Yahweh to act in some way with regard to these entities, and that is the point of this discourse. . . . He is cognizant of his people and intervenes in history on their behalf."[8]

Hamath . . . Tyre and Sidon (9:2). "Hamath was an important Syrian city as well as a province in the Persian Empire. . . . Tyre and Sidon were the two most important cities of Phoenicia."[9]

Take away her possessions and destroy her power (9:4). "Zechariah's words intersected with reality when Alexander the Great placed Tyre under siege, constructing a causeway through the sea to Tyre, which at that time was situated on an island off the coast of the Mediterranean Sea. The prophet Ezekiel envisioned the same event (26:5-6)."[10]

Ashkelon . . . Gaza . . . Ekron . . . Ashdod (9:5-6). Cities of the Philistines.

Will belong to our God and become a clan in Judah (9:7). "The subsequent section (verses 8-10) affirms that these events will come to fruition in the kingdom of Messiah. . . . This section looks far beyond the conquests of Alexander to envision the people of God in all ages. Thus, God protects his people today."[11]

---

3. In 9:9-10, what portrait are we given of Zion's coming ruler?

_____

_____

_____

Lowly and riding on a donkey (9:9). Or, "humble" (ESV, NASB). "We must view Jerusalem's king in contrast to Alexander the Great and the other proud conquerors of history. The reference to

Optional Application: Notice again in Zechariah 9:9 the protection that is promised for God's people, and observe the New Testament promise of this in 2 Thessalonians 3:3, 1 Peter 1:5, and Romans 8:38-39. What does this protection mean personally to you? What freedom does it give you, and what capacities and opportunities—which you can act on *now*?

For Further Study: Reflect again on the message of Zechariah 9:8-9, and the hope created by this text for God's people. How does that hope find fulfillment in the events described in these passages: Matthew 21:1-11; Mark 11:1-11; Luke 19:28-40; John 12:12-19?

111

For Further Study:
What links do you see
between the picture
we see in Zechariah
9:10 and the one
given in Micah
5:10-15? (See also
Zechariah 4:6.)

his riding a beast of burden, not a white char-
ger, underscores this. . . . Jerusalem's king is
of humble mien, yet victorious, and so it has
always been that the church does not effectively
spread the gospel by sword or by arrogance, but
by mirroring the humble spirit of its king and
savior."[12]

***Take away the chariots . . . and the warhorses
. . . and the battle bow will be broken*** (9:10).
"When this king establishes his kingdom, Yahweh will cut off all instruments of war from his
people, freeing them from dependence on their
own might (4:6)."[13]

To the ends of the earth (9:10). "The messianic
king's dominion . . . will be of vast extent,
encompassing people 'from every tribe and
language and people and nation' (Revelation
5:9)."[14]

---

4. What are the most important promises from
God in 9:11-17?

_____

_____

_____

_____

_____

The blood of my covenant (9:11). See Hebrews
13:20.

I will bend Judah as I bend my bow (9:13). "We
learn now how Zion will come to prominence
and power among the nations: Yahweh will use
her as a war bow. He will do this 'for himself';
that is, Zion cannot depend on weapons of war
(9:10) or conquer on her own; it is only as God
uses her as an instrument of war for himself
that he will advance Zion's cause in the arena of
the nations."[15]

---

5. From what they would hear in the prophet's words recorded in chapter 9, what reasons would God's people have to be encouraged?

_____

_____

_____

_____

6. How and why does God judge Judah's rulers in Zechariah 10:1-5?

_____

_____

_____

_____

Ask the LORD for rain (10:1). "Today the church must seek its blessings and power from the Lord, just as Zechariah urged his people to do. Blinded by middle-class values, the people of God may seek their direction in methods that successfully build corporations, but that may neglect biblical principles and fail to reflect the spirit of Christ."[16]

From Judah will come the cornerstone . . . the tent peg . . . the battle bow . . . every ruler (10:4). "From Judah will come . . . 'every' divinely sanctioned king and ultimately the Messiah."[17]

7. What promises for God's people are given in 10:6-12?

_____

_____

_____

_____

In the prophetic text about shepherds in Zechariah 11, "the actors are difficult to identify with certainty ... although the general teaching is clear. The prophet is appointed to be a good shepherd, but because he is rejected he forsakes the flock (verse 9). As a good shepherd, the prophet is a type of the coming messianic Shepherd, Jesus Christ, who came as *the* Good Shepherd and laid down His life for the sheep (John 10:11-18)."[18]

8. Summarize the description being given in 11:1-3 and its significance.

_____

_____

_____

_____

In Zechariah 11, "were the actions assigned to the shepherd carried out as sign-acts, or are the instructions more parable-like, themselves communicating the divine message? Who is the single shepherd who receives these instructions: simply Zechariah, or is a different figure envisaged in verses 15-16? Is it possible, or desirable, to identify the three destroyed shepherds of verse 8? ... Such questions occasion caution at the level of detail. They also have the effect of promoting the fundamental truths enshrined in the text: that the fate of the community for good or ill lies in God's sovereign hands; that God reveals his will to his people; and that God's agents remain responsible for their own actions in response to the divine word."[19]

9. What is the prophet Zechariah called by God to do in 11:4-6, and for what reasons?

_____

_____

_____

_____

_____

Summarize Zechariah's actions and words
    as narrated in 11:7-14, and explain their
    significance.

_____

_____

_____

What is Zechariah called by God to do in
    11:15-17, and for what reasons?

_____

_____

_____

_____

---

*Who will not care . . . or seek . . . or heal . . . or
feed* (11:16). "When one removes 'not' from the
sentence, he has an enlightening description of
a truly effective pastoral ministry in the church
today."[20]

In Zechariah 9–11, what would you select as the
    key verse or passage—one that best captures or
    reflects the dynamics of what these chapters are
    all about?

_____

_____

_____

For Further Study:**
Zechariah 11:13 is
quoted in Matthew
27:9. In its context,
how does Matthew's
quote expand and
intensify the meaning
of Zechariah's words?

13. What do these chapters in Zechariah communicate most to you about the heart and character of God?

_____

_____

_____

_____

14. List any lingering questions you have about Zechariah 9–11.

_____

_____

_____

_____

For the group

You may want to focus your discussion for lesson 9 especially on some of the following issues, themes, and concepts (which are recognized as major overall themes in Zechariah). Which of these are dealt with in some way in chapters 9–11, and how are they further developed there?

- The coming Messiah
- Judgment from God
- Salvation
- Blessing from God
- Events of the future and of the end times
- The promised Messiah
- Holiness

   The following numbered questions in lesson 9 may stimulate your best and most helpful discussion: 2, 4, 7, 12, 13, and 14.
   Remember to look also at the "For Thought and Discussion" questions in the margins.

1. Kenneth L. Barker, "Zechariah," in *Daniel and the Minor Prophets*, The Expositor's Bible Commentary, vol. 7, ed. Frank E. Gabaelein (Grand Rapids, MI: Zondervan, 1985), 656.

2. *NIV Study Bible* (Grand Rapids, MI: Zondervan, 1985), at Zechariah 9:1.
3. *New Geneva Study Bible* (Nashville: Thomas Nelson, 1995), at Zechariah 9:1.
4. Thomas Edward McComiskey, "Zechariah," in *The Minor Prophets* (Grand Rapids, MI: Baker, 2009), 1162.
5. *ESV Study Bible* (Wheaton, IL: Crossway, 2008), at Zechariah 9:1-8.
6. McComiskey, 1159.
7. Barker, 657.
8. McComiskey, 1160.
9. McComiskey, 1160.
10. McComiskey, 1160–1161.
11. McComiskey, 1162–1163.
12. McComiskey, 1166.
13. McComiskey, 1167.
14. McComiskey, 1168.
15. McComiskey, 1171.
16. McComiskey, 1177.
17. Barker, 669.
18. *New Geneva Study Bible*, at Zechariah 11:4-17.
19. *ESV Study Bible*, at Zechariah 11:1-17.
20. Barker, 679.

ZECHARIAH 12–14

The Coming Messiah and His Acceptance

"In this last section of the book, hope for Judah is now tied explicitly to the 'house of David' as various scenarios relating to the future of Jerusalem unfold, signaled by the distinctive phrase 'on that day.'"[1]

1. Summarize the promises made by the Lord to His people in 12:1-9.

_____

_____

_____

_____

On that day (12:3). "This phrase occurs numerous times in chapters 12–14, and indicates the fullness of God's judgment of the world and the final salvation of His people."[2] Notice also 14:1 — "A day of the Lord is coming."

An immovable rock (12:3). Or, "a heavy stone" (ESV, NASB); "a very heave stone" (NKJV). "The earthly Jerusalem of Zechariah's day was a type of the church, the heavenly Jerusalem in which we now live by faith (Hebrews 12:22-24)."[3]

For Thought and Discussion: What are you looking forward to most in eternity?

For Further Study: In Zechariah 12:2, the Lord speaks of "a cup that sends all the surrounding peoples reeling," or "a cup of staggering to all the surrounding peoples" (ESV). Notice how similar language is used in Isaiah 51:17 — though there it is Jerusalem that drinks the cup — an image representing God's wrath. What links do you see also with Jeremiah 25:15-17,27-29 and Ezekiel 23:32-34?

For Further Study:
In Zechariah 12:4, God promises to "keep a watchful eye" over His people. How do you see that promise also in Psalms 32:8 and 33:18?

For Further Study:
Reflect on Zechariah's words regarding "a spirit of grace and supplication" in 12:10. How does this link with prophecies concerning the Holy Spirit in these passages: Isaiah 59:21; Ezekiel 36:26-27; 39:29; Joel 2:28-29?

For Further Study:
In the New Testament, Zechariah 12:10 is quoted in John 19:37 and Revelation 1:7. In their context, how do those passages expand and intensify the meaning of Zechariah's words?

Panic . . . madness (12:4). "In Deuteronomy 28:28, 'panic' (or 'confusion of mind'), 'madness,' and 'blindness' are listed among Israel's curses for disobeying the stipulations of the covenant."[4]

2. In 12:10-14, what does God promise to bring about for David's "house" and the people of Jerusalem—and what significance do you see in this?

_____

_____

_____

_____

A spirit of grace and supplication (12:10). Or, "the Spirit of grace and supplication" (NKJV). "This describes God's gracious Spirit who produces humility in God's people. The Old Testament prophets emphasize that God's renewal of the covenant (Jeremiah 31:31-33) entailed renewal through His Spirit."[5]

They will look on me, the one they have pierced (12:10). "Probably this means 'look to the Messiah as the source of salvation.' Many passages in John's Gospel speak of faith as 'seeing' (John 6:40). The one looked upon in faith is none other than God Himself, who is pierced in the Person of His incarnate Son, the Messiah."[6]

3. Summarize the further promises from God as you see them unfold in 13:1-6, and tell what He will accomplish.

_____

_____

_____

_____

A fountain . . . to cleanse them from sin and impurity (13:1). "The picture of a cleansing fountain indicates the abundance of forgiveness (see Jeremiah 2:13). Ultimately we find that abundance of forgiveness in Jesus and the Spirit (John 7:37-39)."[7]

For Further Study: As another blessing for God's people, Zechariah speaks of "a fountain . . . to cleanse them from sin and impurity (13:1). How is this imagery further developed or prefigured in these passages: Leviticus 14:5; Jeremiah 2:13; Ezekiel 47:1-12; John 7:37-39; Revelation 22:1-2?

"The discourse progresses from the reference to idols to the influence of the false prophets, indicating that their lying prophecies will no longer trouble the people. Not only will Yahweh expel these prophets, but he will also eliminate the motivating energies that led the people astray. Since neither idolatry nor false prophesying appears to have been a major problem in this time, these references to manifestations of Israel's earlier disobedience to God are likely metaphors for the absolute cleansing Yahweh will eventually effect for the nation."[8]

4. What significance do you see in the picture given in 13:7-9, and the promises from God that are associated with it there?

_____

_____

_____

_____

My shepherd (13:7). "The pierced one of 12:10 is to be identified with the shepherd in 13:7."[9]

I will say, "They are my people," and they will say, "The Lord is our God" (13:9). "It is these

121

For Further Study:
Zechariah 13:7 is
quoted in Matthew
26:31 and Mark 14:27.
In their context, how
do those passages
expand and inten-
sify the meaning of
Zechariah's words?

For Further Study:
How does the scene in
Zechariah 14:3-5 com-
pare with what we
see in Acts 1:9-12 and
Revelation 19:11-16?

words that unite the church and the restored
Jewish remnant in a common hope and a
shared inheritance, their experiences in the
world being remarkably parallel."[10]

5. According to the prophetic words in Zechariah
   14:1-11, what can Jerusalem expect to experience in the future?

   _____

   _____

   _____

*East of Jerusalem . . . split in two from east
to west, forming a great valley* (14:4).
"Zechariah's vision . . . resonates with the
upheaval of the earth at the coming of the
Lord depicted elsewhere at Isaiah 40:4 and
Ezekiel 43:2."[11]

Azel (14:5). Its location is uncertain.

The earthquake in the days of Uzziah (14:5).
Mentioned also in Amos 1:1-2.

6. What special significance do you see for the
   statements in 14:9?

   _____

   _____

   _____

"The prophet gives us a glimpse of
heaven in symbols that fall far short of
reality, but whose emotional force reach
a deep level of our comprehension. It is as
though we are observing a stained glass
window depicting a person or event.

The images of colored glass represent objective reality, and while they pulsate with brilliant light, they forever remain symbols. So with apocalyptic, for now we must wait to behold its realities. Beautiful as they are, these figures, like pieces of stained glass diffusing the light of the sun, can only suggest 'what no eye has seen nor ear heard' (1 Corinthians 2:9)."[12]

7. Describe the world events prophesied in 14:12-21.

_____

_____

_____

_____

For Further Study: What links do you see between Zechariah 14:9 and Revelation 21:1-4?

For Further Study: As you reflect on this final scene in Zechariah, in what ways do you see it anticipating the scenes envisioned in Revelation 11:15-19 and 19:11-16?

HOLY TO THE LORD . . . holy to the LORD Almighty (14:20-21). "Here the nature of the messianic kingdom is depicted: It will be characterized by 'holiness.'"[13] See also Zechariah 2:12. "There will be holiness in public life, in religious life, and in private life. Even common things become holy when they are used for God's service. So it is with our lives."[14]

8. In Zechariah 12–14, what would you select as the key verse or passage—one that best captures or reflects the dynamics of what these chapters are all about?

_____

_____

_____

_____

9. What do these chapters in Zechariah communicate most to you about the heart and character of God?

_____

_____

_____

_____

10. List any lingering questions you have about Zechariah 12–14.

_____

_____

_____

_____

Reviewing the book of Zechariah

11. In your study of the book of Zechariah, what have you learned most and appreciated most?

_____

_____

_____

_____

12. Recall again the message of Isaiah 55:10-11 — in the same way God sends rain and snow from the sky to water the earth and nurture life, so also He sends His words to accomplish specific purposes. What would you suggest are God's primary purposes for the message of Zechariah in the lives of His people today?

_____

_____

_____

_____

13. Review again Philippians 4:8 — "Whatever is true, whatever is noble, whatever is right, whatever is pure, whatever is lovely, whatever is admirable — if anything is excellent or praiseworthy — think about such things." As you reflect on all you've read in the book of Zechariah, what stands out to you as being particularly *true*, or *noble*, or *right*, or *pure*, or *lovely*, or *admirable*, or *excellent*, or *praiseworthy* — and therefore well worth thinking more about?

_____

_____

_____

_____

14. Because all of Scripture testifies ultimately of Christ, where does *Jesus* come most in focus for you in this book?

_____

_____

_____

_____

15. In your understanding, what are the strongest ways in which Zechariah points us to humanity's need for Jesus and for what He accomplished in His death and resurrection?

_____

_____

_____

_____

16. Again, recall Paul's reminder in Romans 15:4 — the Old Testament Scriptures can give us endurance and perseverance as well as comfort and encouragement. In your own life, how do you see the book of Zechariah living up to Paul's description? In what ways do they help to

Optional Application: Which verses in Zechariah would be most helpful for you to memorize so you have them always available in your mind and heart for the Holy Spirit to use?

meet your personal needs for both *perseverance* and *encouragement*?

_____

_____

_____

_____

For the group

You may want to focus your discussion for lesson 10 especially on some of the following issues, themes, and concepts (which are recognized as major overall themes in Zechariah). Which of these are dealt with in some way in chapters 12–14, and how are they further developed there?

- The coming Messiah
- Judgment from God
- Salvation
- Blessing from God
- Events of the future and of the end times
- The promised Messiah
- Holiness

The following numbered questions in lesson 10 may stimulate your best and most helpful discussion: 5, 8, 9, and 10.

Allow enough discussion time to look back together and review all of Zechariah as a whole. You can use the numbered questions 11–16 in this lesson to help you do that.

Once more, look also at the questions in the margins under the heading "For Thought and Discussion."

1. *ESV Study Bible* (Wheaton, IL: Crossway, 2008), at Zechariah 12:1–14:21.
2. *New Geneva Study Bible* (Nashville: Thomas Nelson, 1995), at Zechariah 12:3.
3. *New Geneva Study Bible*, at Zechariah 12:3.
4. Kenneth L. Barker, "Zechariah," in *Daniel and the Minor Prophets*, The Expositor's Bible Commentary, vol. 7, ed. Frank E. Gabaelein (Grand Rapids, MI: Zondervan, 1985), 681.

5. *New Geneva Study Bible*, at Zechariah 12:10.
6. *New Geneva Study Bible*, at Zechariah 12:10.
7. *New Geneva Study Bible*, at Zechariah 13:1.
8. Thomas Edward McComiskey, "Zechariah," in *The Minor Prophets* (Grand Rapids, MI: Baker, 2009), 1220.
9. McComiskey, 1223.
10. McComiskey, 1225.
11. *ESV Study Bible*, at Zechariah 14:4.
12. McComiskey, 1234.
13. Barker, 696.
14. Barker, 697.

MALACHI 1–2

Reprimands from God's Heart

"With the book of Malachi, the Old Testament comes to an end. The book therefore has an incipient quality of being a transition from the old covenant to the new covenant, which is still four hundred years off. The dominant note is judgment, as the book informs us regarding what happens when God's people ignore God's rules. The author's implied goal is to lead his readers to reform their lives. This goal is pursued by the prophet's warning his readers about God's impending judgment against sin, and equally by his painting such attractive pictures of God's blessings on those who obey his rules for living that anyone should want to do things God's way. Malachi writes to a backslidden covenant people for whom the life of faith has become a wearisome burden."[1]

"Though Malachi writes to a nation that had been living in the rebuilt Jerusalem for nearly a century after the first exiles had returned, the pictures that he paints of halfhearted religion should strike us as very contemporaneous with our own situation. We can see 'the sins of the saints' laid out to view. Further, the book deals with issues that are common to us — money, marriage, family, contributing to God's work, and many more."[2]

"Malachi either means 'my messenger' or is an abbreviated form of 'the messenger of the LORD.' ... The prophecy is clearly later than those of Haggai and Zechariah....

"Malachi's dialectic style is unique among the prophets. He first makes an assertion, then follows a question from his subjects, and a response proving the original assertion. This style of argumentation or rhetoric became very popular in Judaism."[3]

"Malachi is to be dated about the time of Ezra and Nehemiah.... Some date the book between the coming of Ezra (458 B.C.) and the coming of Nehemiah (445 B.C.). Others place Malachi in the period between Nehemiah's two visits to Jerusalem, about 433 B.C. ...

"The conditions and problems that confronted Ezra and Nehemiah are also found in the prophecy of Malachi. All three spoke out against marriage to foreign wives (for example, Malachi 2:11-15; Nehemiah 13:23-27). They condemned neglect of the tithe (Malachi 3:8-10; Nehemiah 13:10-14). They castigated the evils of a degenerate priesthood (Malachi 1:6–2:9; Nehemiah 13:7,8), and criticized social sins (Malachi 3:5; Nehemiah 5:1-13)."[4]

"God and Malachi wanted a righteous nation, a pure and devoted priesthood, happy homes, God-fearing children, and a people characterized by truth, integrity, generosity, gratitude, fidelity, love, and hope."[5]

"There was one bright spot in the Judean religion in Malachi's time: the people had apparently abandoned formal idolatry once and for all. They may well have continued some of the mentality and practices associated with idolatry but, judging from the complete lack of reference to it in the Books of Ezra, Nehemiah, and Malachi, the practice of idol worship, which had so often corrupted the nation in the past, was now gone. . . .

"The worship of Malachi's time was not heartfelt, however, and the people's offerings were inadequate. Lack of tithing meant lack of true obedience to God.

Optional Application: After His resurrection, when Jesus was explaining Old Testament passages to His disciples, we read that He "opened their minds so they could understand the Scriptures" (Luke 24:45). Ask God to do that kind of work in *your* mind as you study the book of Malachi so you're released and free to learn everything here He wants you to learn—and so you can become as bold and worshipful and faithful as those early disciples of Jesus. Express this desire to Him in prayer.

For Thought and Discussion: How familiar is the book of Malachi to you? What have been your previous impressions of this book?

Freedom from idolatry was not accompanied by vibrant orthodoxy. The earlier era of hope had yielded to a widespread attitude of disaffection with faith in Yahweh. The people to whom Malachi preached were saying, in effect, 'God doesn't seem to care anymore. And if he doesn't care, why should we?'"[6]

1. Reflect once more on Jeremiah 23:29, where God says His Word is "like fire" and "like a hammer"—burning away unclean thoughts and desires in our hearts, as well as crushing and crumbling our spiritual hardness. From your study of Malachi, how do you most want to see the fire-and-hammer power of God's Word at work in your own life? Again, express this longing in a written prayer to God.

   _____

   _____

   _____

   _____

2. Glance ahead through the pages of Malachi and briefly scan all four chapters. What are your overall impressions of the book, including its structure and its themes?

   _____

   _____

   _____

   _____

3. Now turn your focus to the first chapter of Malachi. What are the main points in the message God gives to His people in Malachi 1:2-5?

   _____

   _____

A prophecy: The word of the Lord (1:1). Or, "The burden of the word of the Lord" (NKJV). See also Isaiah 13:1; Nahum 1:1; Habakkuk 1:1; Zechariah 9:1; 12:1.

Edom (1:4). "In the Old Testament, Edom, with its very long and remarkably consistent history of enmity to Israel, is treated virtually as the paradigm of all enemy nations."[7]

The Lord Almighty (1:4). Or, "the Lord of hosts" (ESV, NASB, NKJV). This title for God is used more frequently in Malachi than in any other Old Testament book.

4. What are the main points in the message God gives to His people in 1:6-9?

5. What does 1:10 reveal most about God's mind and heart?

6. What does 1:11 reveal most about God's purpose and intention for the world? (Notice also the closing statement in verse 14.)

For Thought and Discussion: Malachi's prophecy begins with these words from the Lord to His people: "I have loved you" (1:2). To believers today, what is the most common understanding of such a statement from God? And what does such a statement from God mean to our culture in general today?

For Further Study: Malachi 1:2-5 is one of several prophetic passages that deal with Edom (or Seir), the descendants of Esau. What do you learn about the Lord's perspective concerning Edom in the following passages: Isaiah 11:14; 21:11-12; 34:1-17; Jeremiah 25:21; 49:7-22; Lamentations 4:21; Ezekiel 25:12-14; 35:1-15; Joel 3:19; Amos 1:11-12; all of Obadiah?

For Further Study: Notice in Romans 9:13 how Paul quotes from Malachi 1:2. Compare Malachi 1:2-5 with Romans 9; how would you describe the foundational role that Malachi's message plays in Paul's thinking?

For Thought and Discussion: As you reflect on the people's faults as addressed in Malachi 1:12-14, how does this relate to any chronic shortcomings among God's people today?

7. What faults does God find with the people in 1:12-14?

_____

_____

_____

8. What warning does God give His priests in 2:1-3?

_____

_____

_____

9. Explain the main points in the Lord's references to Levi in 2:4-6.

_____

_____

_____

_____

My covenant with Levi (2:4). See also Nehemiah 13:29. "What would the priests have understood by the term 'my covenant with Levi'? On the one hand, it is likely that they would have understood it to mean the whole arrangement that made them priests in Israel. . . . The priests would be aware that certain passages in the law, such as the story of the setting aside of the Levites in Exodus 32:26-29 or Moses' blessing on the Levites in Deuteronomy 33:8-11, were principal in establishing the tribe of Levi as the designated priestly tribe"; in a more focused way, "they would probably have thought in terms of the famous 'covenant of peace' made with Aaron's son Phinehas (Numbers 25:11-13)."[8] See also Jeremiah 33:20-22.

This called for reverence and he revered me (2:5). Or, "It was a covenant of fear, and he feared me" (ESV). "Indicating the serious

134

responsibility of the priests to supervise worship, enforce various provisions of the covenant, and keep the nation holy, that is 'make atonement for the Israelites' (Numbers 25:13). To 'fear' God is to worship and obey him, to make him primary over other interests so that he is honored above all."[9]

True instruction (2:6). "The point is that the priests were servants. They were not authorized to change God's commands or reinterpret them for new times or situations. They were not allowed to be innovators or adapters."[10]

10. Express in your own words the standards that God states for His priests in 2:7.

_____

_____

_____

He is the messenger of the LORD Almighty (2:7). "Priests should have joined with prophets and angels in faithfulness to the Word of God"; this verse "affirms the high calling of the priesthood set out in the Pentateuch, from which the priests had fallen far by Malachi's time."[11]

11. What fault does God find with His priests in 2:8-9?

_____

_____

_____

12. What wrongs committed by God's people are addressed in 2:10-12?

_____

_____

_____

For Further Study:
How do you see the teaching of Malachi 2:7 reinforced and amplified in Jeremiah 18:18, Ezekiel 7:26, and Micah 3:11?

For Further Study:
Think back on the main points concerning the priesthood that have been taught so far in the book of Malachi. How do these points point to the priestly role of Jesus Christ? (Refer especially to how Christ's priestly role is developed in chapters 7 and 8 of Hebrews.)

For Further Study:
Reflecting on Malachi 2:1-9, how do you see the concept of the priesthood enriched by these passages: Exodus 32:26-29; Deuteronomy 33:8-11; Numbers 25:11-13; Jeremiah 33:20-22?

For Thought and Discussion: Again, as you reflect on the people's faults as addressed in Malachi 2:10-12, how does this relate to any chronic shortcomings among God's people today?

For Further Study: As background for Malachi's teaching against religious inter-marriage in 2:10-12, what do you learn from Ezra 9–10 and Nehemiah 13:23-27?

For Further Study: Review the teachings in Malachi 2:10-16 concerning faithfulness, marriage, and divorce. How are these teachings amplified in the words of Jesus Christ in Matthew 19:3-12, as well as the principles given in 1 Corinthians 7:1-16 and 2 Corinthians 6:14-18?

13. What further wrongs on the part of God's people are addressed in 2:13-16?

_____

_____

_____

You weep and wail (2:13). "The Israelites are practicing pagan-style worship. . . . Pagans assumed that the gods could be influenced by loud displays of emotion, intended to demonstrate the earnestness of the worshiper's appeal. . . . It was pagan worship, emphasizing manipulative mourning and misery."[12] "The people's sorrow . . . was for the wrong reasons; they should have been bemoaning their sins rather than their lack of divine acceptance and consequent blessing."[13]

Marriage covenant (2:14). "To violate it was to violate one of the many stipulations that make up the entire covenant (Exodus 19–Deuteronomy 33) and thus to incur any of the curses that Yahweh, the witness-enforcer of that covenant . . . would choose to unleash."[14]

Do not be unfaithful (2:15). "All betrayals, from the slightest unkindness to the grossest injustice, merit God's disapproval. . . . God made monogamous marriage and intends unions to last."[15]

I hate divorce (2:16, footnote). "God succinctly gave his verdict. . . . The covenant made between a man and a woman in the presence of God . . . must be taken with utmost seriousness. 'What God has joined together, let man not separate' was Jesus' way of saying it (Matthew 19:6; Mark 10:9). Not even the man who is a part of that union may make such a separation."[16]

14. What additional wrongs are addressed in 2:17?

_____

_____

_____

_____

_____

Wearied (2:17). "God was tired of hypocrisy, inverted morals, spiritual blindness, and obduracy."[17]

All who do evil are good in the eyes of the LORD (2:17). "Malachi indicates that a considerable number of his contemporaries . . . felt that things had degenerated seriously in their society and that God seemed to be doing nothing about it. . . . The level of sin, crime, and corruption was such that it was *as if* God were encouraging it."[18]

Where is the God of justice? (2:17). "The people—on balance, as a generalization—are overly pessimistic about the intervention of God in the affairs of his people, but . . . when that intervention takes place it will not be what they expect (3:1-5)."[19]

For Further Study: How do the questions posed in Malachi 2:17 compare with the situations you see in these passages: Deuteronomy 32:5, 16-18,28; Psalm 37; 49; 73; Habakkuk 1:2-4,12-17; Romans 1:29-32; 2 Peter 3:4; Revelation 6:9-10?

For Thought and Discussion: Once more, as you reflect on the people's faults and questions as addressed in Malachi 2:13-17, how does this relate to any chronic shortcomings among God's people today?

15. In Malachi 1–2, what would you select as the key verse or passage—one that best captures or reflects the dynamics of what these chapters are all about?

_____

_____

_____

16. What do these chapters in Malachi communicate most to you about the heart and character of God?

_____

_____

_____

137

17. List any lingering questions you have about Malachi 1–2.

_____

_____

_____

_____

For the group

You may want to focus your discussion for lesson 11 especially on some of the following issues, themes, and concepts (which are recognized as major over-all themes in Malachi). Which of these are dealt with in some way in chapters 1–2, and how are they further developed there?

- The power and seriousness of sin
- God's judgment against apostasy and sin
- God's blessing
- God's covenant
- The responsibilities of spiritual leaders

The following numbered questions in lesson 11 may stimulate your best and most helpful discussion: 2, 5, 6, 15, 16, and 17.

Look also at the questions in the margins under the heading "For Thought and Discussion."

1. Leland Ryken and Philip Graham Ryken, eds., *The Literary Study Bible* (Wheaton, IL: Crossway, 2007), introduction to Malachi, "The book at a glance."
2. Ryken and Ryken, introduction to Malachi, "A relevant and contemporary book."
3. *The Complete Word Study Old Testament*, ed. Warren Baker (Chattanooga, TN: AMG, 1994), introduction to Malachi.
4. *New Geneva Study Bible* (Nashville: Thomas Nelson, 1995), introduction to Malachi, "Date and Occasion."
5. Robert L. Alden, "Malachi," in *Daniel and the Minor Prophets*, The Expositor's Bible Commentary, vol. 7, ed. Frank E. Gabaelein (Grand Rapids, MI: Zondervan, 1985), 704.
6. Douglas Stuart, "Malachi," in *The Minor Prophets*, ed. Thomas Edward McComiskey (Grand Rapids, MI: Baker, 2009), 1255.

7. Stuart, 1285.
8. Stuart, 1315.
9. Stuart, 1317–1318.
10. Stuart, 1321.
11. Stuart, 1321.
12. Stuart, 1334.
13. Alden, 717.
14. Stuart, 1338.
15. Alden, 717.
16. Alden, 717.
17. Alden, 719.
18. Stuart, 1348.
19. Stuart, 1347–1348.

MALACHI 3–4
The Coming of the Lord

The opening verses of Malachi 3 continue the discussion begun in the final verse of chapter 2: "Why does God allow such evil as to make it seem like he takes pleasure in the accomplishments of evildoers? And where is he, who is supposed to be the essence of and bringer of justice?"[1]

1. What important aspects in the future of God's people are revealed in 3:1-4?

_____

_____

_____

_____

My messenger, who will prepare the way (3:1). Confirmed in the New Testament as a prophecy concerning John the Baptist, forerunner of Jesus the Messiah. See Matthew 11:10; Mark 1:2; Luke 7:27.

Suddenly the Lord you are seeking will come to his temple; the messenger of the covenant, whom you desire, will come (3:1). This passage "speaks in poetic parallelism, in which two

For Further Study:
Reflect on Malachi's prophetic words in 3:2-3. In the New Testament, how do you see this prophecy confirmed in John 2:14-17, Titus 2:14, and 1 John 3:3?

For Further Study:
Notice again the imagery of purifying fire in Malachi 3:2-3. In what notable ways do you see this imagery expressed in the following passages: Isaiah 29:6; 30:27-30; 66:15-17; Jeremiah 15:14; Ezekiel 22:20-21; 36:5; Joel 1:19-20; 2:3; Nahum 1:6; Zephaniah 1:14-17; Zechariah 13:9?

lines express the same idea in different words. Therefore 'the Lord whom you seek' is the same person as 'the messenger of the covenant in whom you delight,' and thus this coming 'messenger of the covenant' is the same divine being as 'the Lord,' who also is desired and will come. . . . The ministry described in verses 2-4 also indicates the divine nature of this coming Lord."[2] "The phrase 'whom you desire' is interesting. Even in their sin, suggests 2:17, the people longed for deliverance through the Messiah."[3]

Launderer's soap (3:2). Clothes were cleaned "by soaking them in water in which lye had been dissolved, then beating and scrubbing them, and finally rinsing them. This was a separation process . . . separating dirt from fabric. The dirt was taken away and the pure fabric remained, just as in refining the slag was taken away by the heat of the fire and the pure metal remained. Thus fire and lye characterize Yahweh's role on his day. Like fire and lye he will separate what deserves to remain from what is not worthy of keeping."[4] "As a result of that process, God will have an approved and accepted priesthood [3:3-4] to carry out the sacred ministry in a right spirit."[5]

2. What does God promise to do in 3:5?

_____

_____

_____

But do not fear me (3:5). "All the offenders listed in verse 5 are categorized as those who 'do not fear me.' Their sin testified to a lamentable absence of that godly fear that is 'the beginning of knowledge' (Proverbs 1:7)."[6] "Fearing God is not a matter of being terrified of him as if he is always angry, or arbitrary and capricious in his dealings so that one should always be wary of what he might do. Rather, believers fear God's wrath if he is not obeyed. Thus 'fear' functions as a shorthand for 'fearing the consequences of disobeying,' and often for just 'not believing in or taking Yahweh seriously.' "[7]

3. What fault does God find with the people in 3:6-9?

_____

_____

_____

_____

For Further Study:
How is the concept of fearing God in Malachi 3:5 further clarified in the following passages: Psalm 36:1; Proverbs 16:6; Jeremiah 5:22; 32:39; Acts 9:31; 2 Corinthians 7:1?

For Further Study:
As you reflect on the statement of God's unchangeableness in Malachi 3:6, how do you see this doctrine further presented in these passages: Numbers 23:19; 1 Samuel 15:29; Psalm 102:26-27; Lamentations 3:22-23; Hebrews 13:8; James 1:17; Revelation 1:8; 22:13?

I the LORD do not change (3:6). This phrase "implies that God's character and eternal purposes do not change, which gives a solid foundation for his people's faith and hope."[8]

So you . . . are not destroyed (3:6). "Israel deserved destruction for its long history of breaking the covenant, but instead it had not been destroyed. Why? Because God hadn't changed. . . . Yahweh is a blessing God, a forgiving, merciful God. . . . God's unchanging nature allows him to forgive what deserves to be punished. The unchangeableness of God gives foundation to both the truth of Scripture and the promise of eternal life."[9]

4. What corrective action does God command from His people in 3:10?

_____

_____

_____

Pour out so much blessing (3:10). "The promise is, however, corporate, not individual, as are virtually all Old Covenant promises of abundance. No person or family can assume from

143

For Further Study: In the matter of financial giving to the Lord, what links do you see between the teaching in Malachi 3:6-12 and that of Acts 5:1-11 and 2 Corinthians 8 and 9?

For Thought and Discussion: As you reflect on the people's faults being addressed in Malachi 3:6-12, how does this relate to any chronic shortcomings among God's people today?

this oracle that they will get rich from tithing. The nation as a whole can expect, however, to have more than enough food to go around, if it will practice, as a nation, across the board, tithing."[10] God "is inviting his covenant people to realize that if they will return to him and keep his covenant, he will have in store for them good things their own experience could not equal. God's words through his prophet envision something that goes beyond the limited expectations of the little Judean community to which they were first delivered."[11]

---

5. In 3:10-12, what blessings does He promise the people if they obey?

_____

_____

_____

_____

6. What fault does God find with the people in 3:13-15?

_____

_____

_____

_____

It is futile to serve God (3:14). "Their conclusion was falsely based. . . . It followed a line of reasoning characterized by (1) a false assumption, namely, that whatever happens to people in life is a direct result of how they behave, and (2) a false argument from silence, namely, that when God did not act in response to people's expectations, it was the result of his inability to, or his disinterest in doing so. The fact that these two reasoning flaws are extremely common among religious and semireligious people today gives the passage currency."[12]

7. Explain what is being envisioned and what is being promised in 3:16-18.

_____

_____

_____

_____

Those who feared the Lord (3:16). "In sharp contrast to the fault-finding cynics [in 3:13-15], a second group is now mentioned."[13] "They assert, contrary to popular opinion, that Yahweh *has* paid attention and *has* heard."[14]

Scroll of remembrance (3:16). "Almost surely this was a scroll that contained their names as signatories to some sort of statement of their commitment to Yahweh in faith that they were disassociating themselves from the prevailing sins, that his promises were reliable, and that his covenant was to be kept. In other words, it was a covenant renewal document."[15]

_____

8. What are the main features of the future envisioned in Malachi 4:1-3?

_____

_____

_____

9. What is the significance of the command expressed in 4:4?

_____

_____

_____

_____

For Thought and Discussion: Again, as you reflect on the people's faults being addressed in Malachi 3:13-15, how does this relate to any chronic shortcomings among God's people today?

Optional Application: Do you see yourself in this scene depicted in Malachi 3:16-18? If so, in what way? And what relevance does this have for your life today?

For Further Study: Recall how *curse* and *blessing* from the Lord are major themes throughout Malachi. What foundation for the way these themes are developed in Malachi do you see in the teachings given through Moses in Leviticus 26 and Deuteronomy 28?

For Further Study: Reflect further on Malachi 4:1. In the New Testament, how do you see this prophecy confirmed in Matthew 3:10-12 and Revelation 20:11-15? Likewise, how do you see the words of Malachi 4:2 confirmed in Matthew 12:15 and Revelation 21:4?

For Further Study:
The closing words of Malachi — and of the Old Testament — focus on "that great and dreadful day of the LORD" (4:5). Compare and review this concept with what you've learned about it from the prophecies in Isaiah 2:12-21; 13:6-13; Jeremiah 46:10; Ezekiel 7:10-14; Joel 1:15; 2:1,11,31; 3:14; Amos 5:18-20; 8:9-10; Obadiah 15; and Zephaniah 1:7,14-16.

10. What do you see as the greatest significance of God's promises expressed in 4:5-6?

_____

_____

_____

I will send the prophet Elijah to you (4:5). "The New Testament identifies John the Baptist as the fulfillment of Malachi's prophesied Elijah (Matthew 11:10-14; 17:10-13; etc.). When John the Baptist denied that he was Elijah (John 1:21,25), it is possible either that he was denying that he was Elijah in person, or that he rejected not the ministry predicted in Malachi but misguided popular elaborations of this promise based on other notable features in the original Elijah's ministry, especially his many miracles, which pointed more to Christ than to John (John 10:41)."[16] See also Luke 1:17.

"Malachi 3:1 and 4:5-6 together constitute one of Malachi's special contributions to prophecy. They are the most detailed Old Testament contexts indicating that the coming of the Messiah would be preceded by a precursor who would announce the need to prepare for his coming. In this regard Malachi is even more explicit than the more famous verses from Isaiah 40:3-5 that speak of the 'voice' that announces the messianic advent."[17]

11. In Malachi 3–4, what would you select as the key verse or passage — one that best captures or reflects the dynamics of what these chapters are all about?

_____

_____

12. What do these chapters in Malachi communicate most to you about the heart and character of God?

_____

_____

_____

Optional Application: Which verses in the book of Malachi would be most helpful for you to memorize so you have them always available in your mind and heart for the Holy Spirit to use?

13. List any lingering questions you have about Malachi 3–4.

_____

_____

_____

_____

Reviewing the book of Malachi

14. What have you learned most and appreciated most in your study of the book of Malachi?

_____

_____

_____

15. In what ways do you find the message of the book of Malachi to be particularly appropriate for the last book of the Old Testament—the last book *before* Messiah's coming?

_____

_____

_____

16. Recall once more the message of Isaiah 55:10-11 — in the same way God sends rain and snow from the sky to water the earth and nurture life, so also He sends His words to accomplish specific purposes. What would you suggest are God's primary purposes for the message of Malachi in the lives of His people today?

_____

_____

_____

_____

17. Once more, review also the guidelines in Philippians 4:8 — "Whatever is true, whatever is noble, whatever is right, whatever is pure, whatever is lovely, whatever is admirable — if anything is excellent or praiseworthy — think about such things." As you reflect on all you've read in the book of Malachi, what stands out to you as being particularly *true*, or *noble*, or *right*, or *pure*, or *lovely*, or *admirable*, or *excellent*, or *praiseworthy* — and therefore well worth thinking more about?

_____

_____

_____

_____

18. Because all of Scripture testifies ultimately of Christ, where does *Jesus* come most in focus for you in this book?

_____

_____

_____

_____

19. In your understanding, what are the strongest ways in which Malachi points us to humanity's need for Jesus and for what He accomplished in His death and resurrection?

_____

_____

_____

_____

20. Once more, recall Paul's reminder in Romans
    15:4 that the Old Testament Scriptures can
    give us endurance and perseverance as well as
    comfort and encouragement. In your own life,
    how do you see the book of Malachi living up to
    Paul's description? In what ways do they help to
    meet your personal needs for both *perseverance*
    and *encouragement*?

_____

_____

_____

_____

For the group

You may want to focus your discussion for lesson 12
especially on some of the following issues, themes,
and concepts (which are recognized as major overall themes in Malachi). Which of these are dealt
with in some way in chapters 3–4, and how are they
further developed there?

- The power and seriousness of sin
- God's judgment against apostasy and sin
- God's blessing
- God's covenant
- The responsibilities of spiritual leaders

The following numbered questions in lesson 12
may stimulate your best and most helpful discussion:
5, 7, 8, 10, 11, 12, 13, 14, 15, 16, 17, 18, 19, and 20.
Remember to look also at the "For Thought and
Discussion" questions in the margins.

1. Douglas Stuart, "Malachi," in *The Minor Prophets*, ed.
   Thomas Edward McComiskey (Grand Rapids, MI: Baker,
   2009), 1348.

2. *ESV Study Bible* (Wheaton, IL: Crossway, 2008), at Malachi 3:1.
3. Robert L. Alden, "Malachi," in *Daniel and the Minor Prophets*, The Expositor's Bible Commentary, vol. 7, ed. Frank E. Gabaelein (Grand Rapids, MI: Zondervan, 1985), 719.
4. Stuart, 1353.
5. Alden, 719.
6. Alden, 720.
7. Stuart, 1359.
8. *ESV Study Bible*, at Malachi 3:6.
9. Stuart, 1363.
10. Stuart, 1369.
11. Stuart, 1371.
12. Stuart, 1378.
13. *ESV Study Bible*, at Malachi 3:16.
14. Stuart, 1382.
15. Stuart, 1382.
16. *ESV Study Bible*, at Malachi 4:5.
17. Stuart, 1352.

STUDY AIDS

For further information on the material in this study, consider the following sources. Your local Christian bookstore should be able to order any books they do not carry. Most seminary libraries have them, as well as many university and public libraries. If they are out of print, you might be able to find them online.

Commentaries on the final six Minor Prophets

Alden, Robert L. "Haggai" and "Malachi," in *Daniel and the Minor Prophets*, The Expositor's Bible Commentary, vol. 7, ed. Frank E. Gabaelein (Grand Rapids, MI: Zondervan, 1985).

Armerding, Carl E. "Nahum" and "Habakkuk," in *Daniel and the Minor Prophets*, The Expositor's Bible Commentary, vol. 7, ed. Frank E. Gabaelein (Grand Rapids, MI: Zondervan, 1985).

Baker, David W. *Nahum, Habakkuk, Zephaniah: An Introduction and Commentary*, Tyndale Old Testament Commentary, vol. 23b (Downers Grove, IL: InterVarsity, 1988).

Baldwin, Joyce G. *Haggai, Zechariah, Malachi: An Introduction and Commentary*, Tyndale Old Testament Commentary, vol. 24 (Downers Grove, IL: InterVarsity, 1972).

Barker, Kenneth L. "Zechariah," in *Daniel and the Minor Prophets*, The Expositor's Bible Commentary, vol. 7, ed. Frank E. Gabaelein (Grand Rapids, MI: Zondervan, 1985).

Barker, Kenneth L. and Waylon Bailey. *Micah, Nahum, Habakkuk, Zephaniah*, New American Commentary (Nashville: Broadman & Holman, 1998).

Bruce, F. F. "Habakkuk," in *The Minor Prophets*, ed. Thomas Edward McComiskey (Grand Rapids, MI: Baker, 2009).

Calvin, John. *Commentaries on the Twelve Minor Prophets*, 5 vols. (Grand Rapids, MI: Eerdmans, 1950).

Gregory, Bryan R. *Longing for God in an Age of Discouragement: The Gospel According to Zechariah* (Phillipsburg, NJ: P&R, 2010).

Keil, C. F. and F. Delitzsch. *Commentary on the Old Testament: The Minor Prophets*, vol. 10 (Edinburgh, UK: Clark, 1871; Peabody, MA: Hendrickson, 1996).

Longman III, Tremper. "Nahum," in *The Minor Prophets*, ed. Thomas Edward McComiskey (Grand Rapids, MI: Baker, 2009).

Mackay, John. *Haggai, Zechariah and Malachi*, Focus on the Bible (Fearn, Ross-shire, Scotland, UK: Christian Focus, 2003).

McComiskey, Thomas Edward. "Zechariah," in *The Minor Prophets* (Grand Rapids, MI: Baker, 2009).

Motyer, J. Alec. "Zephaniah" and "Haggai," in *The Minor Prophets*, ed. Thomas Edward McComiskey (Grand Rapids, MI: Baker, 2009).

Phillips, Richard D. *Zechariah*, Reformed Expository Commentary (Phillipsburg, NJ: P&R, 2007).

Robertson, O. Palmer. *The Books of Nahum, Habakkuk, and Zephaniah*, New International Commentary on the Old Testament (Grand Rapids, MI: Eerdmans, 1990).

Stuart, Douglas. "Malachi," in *The Minor Prophets*, ed. Thomas Edward McComiskey (Grand Rapids, MI: Baker, 2009).

Verhoef, Pieter. *The Books of Haggai and Malachi*, New International Commentary on the Old Testament (Grand Rapids, MI: Eerdmans, 1987).

Walker, Larry Lee. "Zephaniah," in *Daniel and the Minor Prophets*, The Expositor's Bible Commentary, vol. 7, ed. Frank E. Gabaelein (Grand Rapids, MI: Zondervan, 1985).

Historical background sources and handbooks

Bible study becomes more meaningful when modern Western readers understand the times and places in which the biblical authors lived. *The IVP Bible Background Commentary: Old Testament*, by John H. Walton,

Victor H. Matthews and Mark Chavalas (InterVarsity, 2000), provides insight into the ancient Near Eastern world, its peoples, customs, and geography to help contemporary readers better understand the context in which the Old Testament Scriptures were written.

A **handbook** of biblical customs can also be useful. Some good ones are the time-proven updated classic *Halley's Bible Handbook with the New International Version*, by Henry H. Halley (Zondervan, 2007), and the inexpensive paperback *Manners and Customs in the Bible*, by Victor H. Matthews (Hendrickson, 1991).

Concordances, dictionaries, and encyclopedias

A **concordance** lists words of the Bible alphabetically along with each verse in which the word appears. It lets you do your own word studies. An *exhaustive* concordance lists every word used in a given translation, while an *abridged* or *complete* concordance omits either some words, some occurrences of the word, or both.

Two of the best exhaustive concordances are *Strong's Exhaustive Concordance* and *The Strongest NIV Exhaustive Concordance*. *Strong's* is available based on the King James Version of the Bible and the New American Standard Bible. *Strong's* has an index that shows which Greek or Hebrew word is used in a given English verse. The NIV concordance does the same thing except it also includes an index for Aramaic words in the original texts from which the NIV was translated. However, neither concordance requires knowledge of the original languages.

A **Bible dictionary** or **Bible encyclopedia** alphabetically lists articles about people, places, doctrines, important words, customs, and geography of the Bible.

Holman Illustrated Bible Dictionary, by C. Brand, C. W. Draper, and A. England (B&H, 2003), offers more than seven hundred color photos, illustrations, and charts; sixty full-color maps; and up-to-date archeological findings—along with exhaustive definitions of people, places, things, and events—and deals with every subject in the Bible. It uses a variety of Bible translations and is the only dictionary that includes the HCSB, NIV, KJV, RSV, NRSV, REB, NASB, ESV, and TEV.

The New Unger's Bible Dictionary, Revised and Expanded, by Merrill F. Unger (Moody, 2006), has been a best seller for almost fifty years. Its 6,700-plus entries reflect the most current scholarship, and more than 1.2 million words are supplemented with detailed essays, colorful photography and maps, and dozens of charts and illustrations to enhance your understanding of God's Word. Based on the New American Standard Bible.

The Zondervan Encyclopedia of the Bible, edited by Moisés Silva and Merrill C. Tenney (Zondervan, 2008), is excellent and exhaustive. However, its five 1,000-page volumes are a financial investment, so all but very serious students may prefer to use it at a church, public, college, or seminary library.

Unlike a Bible dictionary in the above sense, *Vine's Complete Expository Dictionary of Old and New Testament Words*, by W. E. Vine, Merrill F. Unger, and William White Jr. (Thomas Nelson, 1996), alphabetically lists major words used in the King James Version and defines each Old Testament Hebrew or New Testament Greek word the KJV translates with that English word. *Vine's* lists verse references where that Hebrew or Greek word appears so that you can do your own cross-references and word studies without knowing the original languages.

The Brown-Driver-Briggs Hebrew and English Lexicon by Francis Brown, C. Briggs, and S. R. Driver (Hendrickson, 1996), is probably the most respected and comprehensive Bible lexicon for Old Testament studies. *BDB* gives not only dictionary definitions for each word but relates each word to its Old Testament usage and categorizes its nuances of meaning.

Bible atlases and map books

A **Bible atlas** can be a great aid to understanding what is going on in a book of the Bible and how geography affected events. Here are a few good choices:

The Hammond Atlas of Bible Lands (Langenscheidt, 2007) packs a ton of resources into just sixty-four pages. It includes maps, of course, but also photographs, illustrations, and a comprehensive timeline. It offers an introduction to the unique geography of the Holy Land, including terrain, trade routes, vegetation, and climate information.

The New Moody Atlas of the Bible, by Barry J. Beitzel (Moody, 2009), is scholarly, very evangelical, and full of theological text, indexes, and references. Beitzel shows vividly how God prepared the land of Israel perfectly for the acts of salvation He was going to accomplish in it.

Then and Now Bible Maps Insert (Rose, 2008) is a nifty paperback size just right to fit inside your Bible cover. Only forty-four pages long, it features clear plastic overlays of modern-day cities and countries so you can see what nation or city now occupies the Bible setting you are reading about. Every major city of the Bible is included.

For small-group leaders

Discipleship Journal's Best Small-Group Ideas, Volumes 1 and 2 (NavPress, 2005). Each volume is packed with 101 of the best hands-on tips and group-building principles from *Discipleship Journal's* "Small Group Letter" and "DJ Plus" as well as articles from the magazine. They will help you inject new passion into the life of your small group.

Donahue, Bill. *Leading Life-Changing Small Groups* (Zondervan, 2002). This comprehensive resource is packed with information, practical tips, and insights that will teach you about small-group philosophy and structure, discipleship, conducting meetings, and more.

McBride, Neal F. *How to Build a Small-Groups Ministry* (NavPress, 1994). This is a time-proven, hands-on workbook for pastors and lay leaders that includes everything you need to know to develop a plan that fits your unique church. Through basic principles, case studies, and worksheets, McBride leads you through twelve logical steps for organizing and administering a small-groups ministry.

McBride, Neal F. *How to Lead Small Groups* (NavPress, 1990). This book covers leadership skills for all kinds of small groups: Bible study, fellowship, task, and support groups. It's filled with step-by-step guidance and practical exercises to help you grasp the critical aspects of small-group leadership and dynamics.

Miller, Tara and Jenn Peppers. *Finding the Flow: A Guide for Leading Small Groups and Gatherings* (IVP Connect, 2008). *Finding the Flow* offers a fresh take on leading small groups by seeking to develop the leader's small-group facilitation skills.

Bible study methods

Discipleship Journal's Best Bible Study Methods (NavPress, 2002). This is a collection of thirty-two creative ways to explore Scripture that will help you enjoy studying God's Word more.

Hendricks, Howard and William Hendricks. *Living by the Book: The Art and Science of Reading the Bible* (Moody, 2007). *Living by the Book* offers a practical three-step process that will help you master simple yet effective inductive methods of observation, interpretation, and application that will make all the difference in your time with God's Word. A workbook by the same title is also available to go along with the book.

The Navigator Bible Studies Handbook (NavPress, 1994). This resource teaches the underlying principles for doing good inductive Bible study, including instructions on doing question-and-answer studies, verse-analysis studies, chapter-analysis studies, and topical studies.

Warren, Rick. *Rick Warren's Bible Study Methods: Twelve Ways You Can Unlock God's Word* (HarperCollins, 2006). Warren offers simple, step-by-step instructions, guiding you through twelve approaches to studying the Bible for yourself with the goal of becoming more like Jesus.

N A V E S S E N T I A L S

Voices of The Navigators—Past, Present, and Future

NavEssentials offer core Navigator messages from such authors as Jim Downing, LeRoy Eims, Mike Treneer, and more — at an affordable price. This new series will deeply influence generations in the movement of discipleship. Learn from the old and new messages of The Navigators how powerful and transformational the life of a disciple truly is.

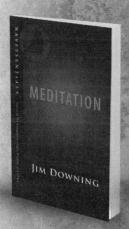

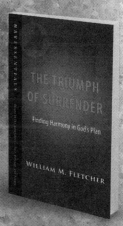

Meditation
by Jim Downing
9781615217250 | $5.00

Advancing the Gospel
by Mike Treneer
9781617471575 | $5.00

The Triumph of Surrender
by William M. Fletcher
9781615219070 | $5.00

Available wherever books are sold.   NAVPRESS ⬤